BFI FILM CL
. . . .
Rob Wh
S E R I E S E L

Edward Buscombe, Colin MacCabe and David Meeker
S E R I E S   C O N S U L T A N T S

Cinema is a fragile medium. Many of the great films now exist, if at all, in damaged or incomplete prints. Concerned about the deterioration in the physical state of our film heritage, the National Film and Television Archive, part of the British Film Institute's Collections Department, has compiled a list of 360 key works in the history of the cinema. The long-term goal of the Archive is to build a collection of perfect showprints of these films, which will then be screened regularly at the National Film Theatre in London in a year-round repertory.

BFI Film Classics is a series of books intended to introduce, inter-pret and honour these 360 films. Critics, scholars, novelists and those distinguished in the arts have been invited to write on a film of their choice, drawn from the Archive's list. The numerous illustrations have been made specially from the Archive's own prints.

With new titles published each year, the BFI Film Classics series is a unique, authoritative and highly readable guide to the masterpieces of world cinema.

The best movie publishing idea of the [past] decade.
Philip French, *Observer*

A remarkable series which does all kinds of varied and divergent things.
Michael Wood, *Sight and Sound*

Exquisitely dimensioned ... magnificently concentrated examples of freeform critical poetry.
Uncut

Shooting into the dumpster for the fight scene. Cassavetes shot silent and called out directions as he filmed (© Sam Shaw)

BFI FILM CLASSICS

SHADOWS

....

Ray Carney

 Publishing

First published in 2001 by the
BRITISH FILM INSTITUTE
21 Stephen Street, London W1P 2LN

The British Film Institute
promotes greater understanding
and appreciation of, and
access to, film and moving image
culture in the UK.

British Library Cataloguing-in-Publication Data
A catalogue record for this book is available from the British Library

ISBN 0–85170–835–8

Series design by
Andrew Barron & Collis Clements Associates

Typeset in Fournier and Franklin Gothic by
D R Bungay Associates, Burghfield, Berks

Printed in Great Britain by The Cromwell Press, Trowbridge, Wiltshire

CONTENTS

. . . .

Acknowledgments *6*

'Shadows' *7*

Appendix:
A Comparison of the Two Versions of 'Shadows' *72*

Notes *81*

Credits *86*

ACKNOWLEDGMENTS
. . . .

The book originated in a conversation with John Cassavetes where he mentioned that no one knew 'the real story' of the making of *Shadows* and then told me about Robert Alan Aurthur's contribution and teased me with a few other tantalising facts. Thus began a series of conversations over a period of a decade with nine individuals who were involved with the making of the film from the beginning: Sam Shaw, Lelia Goldoni, Maurice McEndree, Burt Lane, Hugh Hurd, Erich Kollmar, David Pokotilow, Tony Ray and George O'Halloran. Shaw, Goldoni, McEndree and Lane cumulatively spent more than two hundred hours responding to questions. Goldoni kindly read and fact-checked the final text.

These interactions were supplemented by conversations with others whose involvement with the film was more distant or of shorter duration. Tom Bower and Meta Shaw, students at the Variety Arts workshop, described the atmosphere and activities. Seymour Cassel, who joined the crew halfway through the first shoot and was not present for all of it, described what he remembered. Al Ruban didn't meet Cassavetes until after the first version had been screened, and was only involved in part of the reshoot, but recounted several events from 1959. Jonas Mekas, Amos Vogel, and Gideon Bachmann relayed memories of some of the early screenings.

I am also indebted to a large number of film curators, programmers, and university faculty members who sponsored Cassavetes-related events which I curated or moderated. Most notable are Lisa Philips and John Hanhardt, formerly at the Whitney Museum of American Art, New York, for whom I curated the film and video component of the Whitney's 'Beat Culture and the New America' show and who commissioned two essays about *Shadows* and other Beat works for the show's catalogue, and Joy Gould Boyum of the School of Education, New York University, who sponsored a reunion of *Shadows*' cast and crew which I organised and moderated.

Gena Rowlands, representing the estate of John Cassavetes, kindly provided permission for the use of Cassavetes' words.

Diane Cherkerzian, as always, did more than could ever be adequately acknowledged.

'SHADOWS'

. . . .

'The film you have just seen was an improvisation'

In the spring of 1960, John Cassavetes was a young actor who had played a series of undistinguished roles in a string of low-budget B-movies and television shows. Six months later, he was being hailed as one of the most promising directors in the world. In July, his first film, *Shadows*, played to standing-room-only audiences at the National Film Theatre's 'Beat, Square and Cool Festival'. In August, it played out of competition at the Venice Film Festival and received a special critics' citation. In September, it played at a special screening at the Cinémathèque Française in Paris, where approximately a thousand people were turned away from the box office. In early October, it played in the London Film Festival, to rave reviews and a sustained ovation from the audience. And a week later, on 14 October, it opened at London's Academy Cinema, playing to capacity crowds and taking in more money than any film in the theatre's twenty-five year history.

Cassavetes attended the opening with members of the cast and crew, and was over the moon with delight. His 16mm movie, made for

$40,000 with unknown actors (none of whom had ever played an important film role before) was hailed by one critic as 'a major breakthrough in the art of the cinema'. Another wrote: 'I unhesitatingly pronounce *Shadows* the most artistically satisfying and exciting film I have seen in a decade'. Newspapers from *The Times* and *Observer* to the *Daily Mirror* and *Daily Express* ran laudatory reviews, and the most important film magazine of the era, *Sight and Sound*, devoted sections of three successive issues (autumn 1960, winter 1960–1, and spring 1961) to discussions of the film and an interview with the film-maker.

What most captivated the critics was the spontaneity and speed with which the movie had been made. *Shadows* itself ended with the declaration: 'The film you have just seen was an improvisation', and the press pack proudly proclaimed: 'Not one word of [the] dialogue was written. Not one scene was detailed in script.' It described how the crew had 'grabbed' most of the footage on New York streets: 'They concealed their camera in subway entrances, restaurant windows, the backs of trucks.' When interviewers asked Cassavetes to tell them more, he not only bragged that the whole project had been accomplished in forty-two days and nights, but said that it could have been done even more quickly if he had not occasionally had to suspend work while his young actors went off to appear in other projects to earn money. He told them the sound was a little rough because it was completely 'live' – unlike a typical studio production, nothing had been looped or 'faked'. Then he regaled them with stories like the one about how the police had tried to shut down the 'outlaw' production – at one point firing a gun over the actors' heads to stop a scene.

What no one suspected was that it was a pack of lies. Most of *Shadows* was not shot on 'location' or on the streets of New York, but on a stage. No policeman had ever fired a gun at the actors – or over their heads. More than half of the sound was not 'live', but had been dubbed, looped or otherwise manipulated during the editing process. And, far from being a six-weeks' wonder, *Shadows* had taken almost three years to make. Finally, notwithstanding the final title card, at least two-thirds of the film was *not* an improvisation, but was written by Cassavetes in collaboration with a professional Hollywood screenwriter. Every one of the scenes the critics praised in his 'masterpiece of improvisation' had been scripted.

'I used to walk around angry all the time' [1]
To tell the true story of *Shadows* one must go back a decade before the London events, to March 1950 when Cassavetes graduated from the

American Academy of Dramatic Arts (AADA). It was the beginning of years of unhappiness. The aspiring actor was completely unable to get meaningful work, spending his days futilely making the rounds of casting offices and his evenings hanging out with his two roommates, going to bars, and picking up women. It was a time of deep frustration and simmering anger. Cassavetes drifted, bar-hopped, and grew ever more bitter. As the fourth anniversary of his graduation approached, he had not played a single role with more than five lines of dialogue.

It wasn't until the spring of 1954 that he got his first important job. His life radically changed in the next three years. His salary sky-rocketed to around $25,000 a year (equivalent to at least ten times that amount in contemporary dollars), he moved into an upper East Side penthouse, and by mid-1956 his acting career was successful beyond his wildest dreams of a few years before. But he was still angry and disillusioned. He felt the roles offered to him were clichés. Then there were the creative conditions – particularly in film. The entire production seemed to be arranged more for the convenience of the cameraman, the lighting technicians, and the focus pullers, than to allow the actor to give a decent performance. Scenes were broken up into short takes and close-ups, during which the other actors with whom Cassavetes would be nominally interacting might not even be present. Actors' movements were constrained to hit lighting and focus 'marks'. Finally, and most stifling of all, at least in Hollywood, was the size and bureaucratic sprawl of the production. When so many people were involved, it was impossible for any one individual to have very much creative input. The actor became a cog in a well-oiled machine.

At a point at which other actors might have been counting their blessings and dabbling in the stock market, Cassavetes looked at the future with dread. He dreamed of doing something freer, more creative and more daring; but he had no idea how to make it happen.

'I found other people it drove crazy too'

As an actor you don't get the freedom to function the way you'd like to. I know I never got the lines I wanted under other directors. I couldn't stand the idea of sitting around for a couple of years waiting for the phone to ring. It drove me crazy. So I found other people that it drove crazy too, and we started working together. It saved me from going off the deep end.

In late 1955, Cassavetes and another unemployed AADA graduate named Burt Lane began a series of impromptu gatherings with actor friends to read scenes a couple evenings a week. It was fun and the two men got the idea to rent a regular space to meet. After a little shopping around, they settled on the Variety Arts building, which was located in a low-rent section of Manhattan between Broadway and 8th Avenue at 225 West 46th Street. Though the space is now a parking lot, at the time it was a dilapidated four-storey building given over to rehearsal rooms. Cassavetes and Lane started in a couple of rooms on an upper floor, but shortly afterwards moved down to the ground floor, which was empty and available for around $800 a month. In the spring of 1956, they moved in and announced the opening of the 'Cassavetes-Lane Drama Workshop'.

A personal event conspired to push Cassavetes into the project. In October 1955, his wife, Gena Rowlands, began preparing for her Broadway début playing opposite Edward G. Robinson in Paddy Chayefsky's *The Middle of the Night*. From December on, she was absolutely consumed with preparations, and from February 1956 on, was on stage almost every single evening and several afternoons a week.[2] Cassavetes got tired of sitting home alone or in bars. The workshop would be something to do in the evenings.

There was a lot of work to be done. When they moved into the ground floor, it was a complete wreck. Lane and a handful of so-called 'students' (who were mainly just friends and other hangers-on) spent months cleaning up the space, erecting walls to divide it into smaller units, and building a raised rehearsal stage in the newly created front room. It was all extremely small, dirty and dingy – 'a real *New York* space!' in the words of one of the actors from California. The stage was tiny, interrupted at one end by a stanchion that supported the floor above, had a ceiling only 15 ft. high (meaning there were no flies for scenery or curtains to be drawn up into), and was illuminated by a single spotlight hanging from the ceiling. Lane arranged four rows of folding chairs in front to seat a maximum audience of approximately thirty, which was at that point at least twenty more than they needed. By erecting interior walls, Lane and his helpers created three or four smaller rooms, which would eventually be used as a second classroom, a front office and an editing suite once *Shadows* got underway. Nothing was soundproofed, so the thumps of dance classes on the floors above reverberated throughout the workshop all day long.

Workshop meetings were extremely informal. Cassavetes, Lane

and the young actors got together only a few evenings a week, with many hiatuses: for example, in the spring of 1956, when both Cassavetes and Lane went to Cuba to work on *Affair in Havana* for six weeks, and in the summer of 1956, when Cassavetes went off to act in regional theatre in Connecticut, the workshop simply shut down. The understanding was that as a 'name' actor and a draw, Cassavetes would teach a 'professional' class and Lane the 'intermediate' and 'beginner' classes. Although the two men did their best to drum up students, and practically begged everyone they knew to attend, only a few friends took them up on the offer – so that the initial groups consisted of only about ten members each, none of whom had very much prior experience. Even those in Cassavetes' 'professional' group, who would later become the nucleus of *Shadows*' cast, were not really 'professionals'.

Cassavetes did everything he could to build up membership of his group, and was not above a certain amount of deceit to do it. He was full of vague promises about getting his students agents and work. He attempted to entice friends to join his group by suspending tuition fees and telling them that he wanted them to be teachers, not students. Hugh Hurd and Tony Ray both told me they came in believing that they could offer acting classes. Lelia Goldoni, who had studied with Lester Horton,

A Cassavetean joke from *Staccato*. At 6 minutes and 45 seconds into *Shadows*, Ben walks exactly where Cassavetes does here

was told she could teach dance and movement. Cassavetes told a recent graduate of Sanford Meisner's Neighborhood Playhouse, Tom Gilson, that he would pay him to fill in for him when he too busy acting to teach. The promises were conveniently forgotten once everyone showed up. But if it came down to who was using whom, it worked both ways. The members of Cassavetes' group joined more out of a hope that the connection with him might lead to a paying job than out of a desire to take classes with him.

Cassavetes saw no conflict between the two goals. Personal development and professional advancement could go hand in hand. His idea was periodically to showcase his young actors' talents in front of invited groups of agents, producers and directors. The Actors Studio did it; but unfortunately when he and Lane tried to do the same thing, it was a complete flop. Phone calls were made; letters were written; but no one showed up but the actors. Cassavetes discovered he simply did not have the drawing power that Strasberg did. The Actors Studio had nothing to fear from the Variety Arts workshop.

Madness and the Method

The contrast with the Studio stung Cassavetes all the more, since he had both personal and intellectual differences with Strasberg. He was resentful about the power the Studio exerted over New York casting directors and was convinced that his not being an alumnus was what had prevented him from being hired early in his career. He was also scornful of what he called the 'guru' aspects of the Studio, and despised the cult of personality that had grown up around Strasberg (scorning it as only someone half envious of it would). Cassavetes and Lane pointedly described their own approach to students as being 'anti-guru'. Cassavetes believed that although figures like Clift, Brando and Dean had had a salutary influence on acting in the late 1940s and early 50s, by the middle of the decade the Method had hardened into a received style that was as rigid, unimaginative and boring as the styles it had replaced ten years earlier. The slouch, shuffle, furrow and stammer had been turned into recipes for profundity.

Acting as Playing

As luck would have it, shortly after the workshop got underway, Cassavetes was invited to audition for the Actors Studio.[3] But instead of being flattered, he was irritated, since he felt that when he had needed the Studio five years earlier, it would not talk to him, but now that he was successful it was suddenly interested. He decided to play a trick on

Strasberg. He brought Lane along to the audition and told Strasberg the two men were going to do a scene from a new play entitled *Bill Bower's Boys* about two black siblings 'passing' for white. But there was no play. Cassavetes and Lane simply improvised a scene on the spot (after having done a single quick run-through earlier that morning).

To Cassavetes' delight and Lane's amazement, Strasberg fell for the ruse. He believed the story, loved the piece and performance, and offered Cassavetes immediate admission to the Studio. Cassavetes then sprang the second part of the trap. He told Strasberg a sob story about how little money he had and that he could not afford to attend. When Strasberg agreed to give him a scholarship, Cassavetes gleefully revealed it all, and told Strasberg that he was not interested in studying under someone who obviously knew nothing about acting, since he couldn't see through any of the lies that had been inflicted on him.

It was a typical Cassavetes prank, but it also summed up the philosophical difference between his approach to acting and Strasberg's. The Studio's sense of acting was that it was something serious, laboured and earnest. Cassavetes' understanding was that acting was a form of play. It could be zany, comical and madcap. In Strasberg's vision, the theatre was a church; in Cassavetes', it was a playground. While the Actors Studio specialised in moody, broody anguish, Cassavetes felt that acting was fundamentally an expression of joy and exuberance.

The Mask of Personality

There was another difference between Strasberg on the one hand and Lane and Cassavetes on the other. As Lane told an interviewer in 1958, the problem with the Method was that:

> In focusing on core emotions, it removed the masks of the characters and deprived them of personalities. In real life, we rarely act directly from our emotions. Feeling is simply the first link in a chain. It is followed by an adjustment of the individual to the situation and to the other people involved in it, and this in turn leads to the projection of an attitude which initiates the involvement with other persons. On top of that, there is the problem of characterisation. Actors who are preoccupied with themselves – with examining and recalling their own innermost experiences – cannot properly interact with others on stage, much less approximate the interactions of others with themselves. Since most dramatic conflict arises either from characters trying to get behind the personality masks of others, or from trying to prevent

others from seeing through their own masks, a method which neglects the recreation of a character's mask is essentially destructive of dramatic values.[4]

Cassavetes drew many of his fundamental dramatic concepts from Lane, and Lane's notion that characters wear 'personality masks' informs all of Cassavetes' work. Not only are there explicit references to masks in *Shadows* in the scene in the Museum of Modern Art sculpture garden and in the shot that begins the post-coital scene between Lelia and Tony, but it is not an overstatement to say that the fundamental drama of the film is generated by the mask each character wears.[5]

Cassavetes felt that the appeal of the Method arose from the fact that actors *didn't* have to create and maintain a mask or a sharply defined character. The actor was allowed to fill the character up with his own private fantasies and emotions. Rather than going out of himself to become someone else, the actor defined the character in terms of his own personal needs and desires. This flattered the actor because it told him that acting was ultimately about *himself*. The result, in Cassavetes' and Lane's view, was lazy, sentimental, narcissistic acting. In ignoring the 'mask' – the obliquity and ulteriority emotional expression took on as it passed through the prism of character – the Actors Studio radically simplified both acting and life. The outside of life dropped away; characters became all inside. The individual's social expressions of himself – the complex algebra of bodily, gestural and verbal interaction – ceased to matter or even be represented on stage. The dismissive term Cassavetes and Lane used to describe the Method was 'organized introversion'. Since one of Cassavetes' fundamental dramatic beliefs was that individuals are social beings, there could be no greater loss. To understand life in terms of simple states of feeling rather than complex social expressions of those feelings was to trivialise it – dramatically and humanly.

'When are we going to get any real work?'

By January 1957 Cassavetes' class consisted of about twenty students. They loved what they were doing, but kept putting pressure on Cassavetes to help them get 'real work'. They knew they couldn't keep experimenting with scenes for the rest of their lives.

At a break in one of the classes, Cassavetes went around and whispered in the ears of ten of his best students that they should show up on Sunday afternoon at 3 p.m. for a special session. Since they had never

In the 1959 reshoot, Cassavetes somewhat self-consciously incorporated references to 'masks' to thematise the 'mask-wearing' issue

met on a Sunday before, and since Cassavetes did the whole thing in his trademark 'mysterioso' manner, refusing to answer questions about what was going on or why he had picked certain people and left out others, the actors were abuzz with expectation.

'An improvisation that sprang to life'
When the group convened a few days later, Cassavetes outlined a detailed scene, which he asked the actors to improvise. He didn't give them any specific dialogue, but, as given circumstances, specified the personalities of the characters and a complex situation in which they found themselves. Three of the actors would play siblings in a African-American family consisting of two brothers and a sister living together in a New York apartment. The 'baby sister' (a role that was to have been played by an aspiring actress named Janet Conway but would be taken over by Lelia Goldoni) was young, light-skinned and fairly innocent. Her light-skinned younger brother (played by Ben Carruthers) was much more conscious of racial issues, but 'passing' for white and unresolved about his real identity. The darker, older brother (played by Hugh Hurd) was comfortable with his racial situation but frustrated in his job and hard-pressed as a wage-earner supporting the family. Another actor (Tom Gilson was Cassavetes' initial choice, but he was later replaced by Tony Ray) would play a 'make-out artist' who had just seduced the sister without being aware of her race. The specific moment Cassavetes asked the actors to work on was when the girl had just had sex for the first time with the white boy and returned with him to her apartment where her light-skinned brother, Ben, was hanging out with his buddies. After some awkward interaction, Ben and his friends left and the older dark-skinned brother, Hugh, entered the apartment accompanied by his equally dark-skinned manager (played by Rupert Crosse), at which point the white boy suddenly realised that the girl was black. Cassavetes asked the actors to improvise how the situation might play out.

Cassavetes brushed away every objection to the premise. When Hugh said that nobody would believe that Lelia was his sister he replied, 'We'll let the audience worry about the mother and father.' When Lelia Goldoni raised a similar concern he told her, 'if they can believe it even for a second, maybe they'll start asking what being Negro means and start thinking about the whole concept'. But once the concerns were allayed, the event was magical. According to Lelia Goldoni, from the moment Ben playfully said, 'Hi sister!' the scene caught fire. It was the most exciting improvisation they had ever done, and went on for more than three hours.

By tapping into the sex-and-race issue, Cassavetes created an unusually powerful experience. It's difficult to recapture the sensitive nature of the dramatic premise at this point in history, but suffice it to say that although interracial friendship was accepted in intellectual and artistic circles in the late 50s, interracial dating was still fairly taboo, and interracial sexual relations were almost unmentionable. Cassavetes deliberately created a situation about which even 'progressive' young people had mixed feelings.[6] Everyone in the workshop believed in the abstract in racial integration and equality; but at the same time most of them realised that they themselves might be upset if they found themselves or their sister in this situation. The clash between what they knew to be 'correct and acceptable' codes of social behaviour and their sense of what their true feelings might actually be was the source of the scene's power. Since the characters were acting out of states of primordial fear and insecurity, they could not rely on polite, formulaic responses to get through the moment. There was no easy interactional path or resolution which could still be truthful to the emotional pain and awkwardness of the moment.[7]

Not Pretending but Being
Another reason the initial improvisation and many of the other scenes that evolved from it had such a galvanising effect on the actors was that they were quarried from their off-screen personalities and experiences. Throughout his career Cassavetes played a deep game in this respect. He based things on his actors' personalities and real-life experiences, yet changed the surface details enough so that they weren't entirely aware of what was going on. They didn't realise that they were playing themselves because the characters were different from them in superficial respects. The result was that even as the roles tapped into deep structures of feeling and personality that enriched the performances and made them profoundly revealing, the actors played them in an unselfconscious and unguarded way.

Hugh is a jazz singer whose career is stagnating, and Hugh Hurd at the time was an aspiring opera singer whose career had not progressed the way he wanted it to. He plays an older brother who looks out for his younger siblings, and, in fact, Hurd actually functioned as a 'big brother' to the workshop's younger actors (and particularly to Lelia Goldoni). Even a relatively trivial detail, like the fact that Hugh's character is comically late everywhere he goes, is drawn from life. Hurd was notorious for being the last one to show up everywhere. Ben Carruthers plays a character who is 'passing', and he was, in fact, one-eighth black (with a mix of Puerto Rican), unresolved about his racial identity, and 'passed' in many situations. Carruthers' character is a bit of a poser, more of a talker than a doer, and by all accounts, so was he. (Like his character, who clearly would rather talk trumpet than play it, Carruthers fantasised about being a jazz musician, while not actually playing an instrument.) Lelia Goldoni was perceived by many of the members of the workshop as a bit of a flirt, with her head in the clouds, and an inflated notion of herself. And she was, in fact, involved in an interracial dating situation (marrying Ben Carruthers a few months after the first shoot of *Shadows* was completed). Tony Ray was, in fact, infatuated with Lelia; and, more importantly, was a bit of a fraud. As Hugh Hurd put it: 'Tony was very closed up. It was very hard to get to him or to get him to be emotionally open. That then became his character. John made use of everything.'

The overlap of the actors' and characters' lives undoubtedly contributed to the authenticity of the performances. The on-screen tenderness between Lelia and Hugh is convincing precisely because Lelia Goldoni and Hugh Hurd did feel genuinely tender toward each other. Ben's posturing or Tony's Don Juanism are convincing because these qualities were large parts of who they really were. Acting was not pretending, but being. What you really were, what you really felt, became your character. Everything in your life and experiences could be used.

'The mistakes in your life are assets on film'

> When a scene plays awkwardly or something goes wrong, I don't criticize it, change it, or call cut. I look at it and say, alright, it's not exactly the right reading, but life doesn't always have the right meaning. We stutter, we stammer through life. We sometimes say things we're sorry for later. We make fools of ourselves constantly. In life this is frowned upon, but in a movie this is revealing. The mistakes that you make in your own life, in your own personality, are assets on the film. So if I can just convince somebody not to clean themselves up, and not to be someone they're not and just be what they are in a given circumstance, that's all that acting is to me.

Another way to understand Cassavetes' 'use' of his actors' actual personalities is to say that Cassavetes deliberately retained their personal shortcomings and eccentricities in their performances. If Tony took himself too seriously as a human being and an actor (as is apparent from the pretentious pauses he inserts in his replies during the pre- and post-coital scenes), that became his character. If Jack Ackerman nervously twitched and shrugged his way through his role (as he does), that became his character. If Cassavetes had had his young actors mimic the smoothness and professionalism of Hollywood performance, 'cleaning themselves up', he would have eliminated the very flaws and imperfections that made them interesting as people.

Autobiographical Film-making

> There were three of us in one room … going around looking for jobs … I didn't do too well … My first real job wasn't until years after I graduated. I spent years making the rounds by day, and chasing women and liquor at night … Since none of us had any money, we had to use our wits. We had to get girls to give us their apartment, come in and cook for us, bring food over. We found that trying to get along with actresses who are broke too is no good. We had to go out and find people who weren't actresses – airline hostesses, women who worked in grocery stores, who could pick up some groceries for us. We had to find librarians, to get a better book collection, and stuff like that. We had a wonderful time. I couldn't wait for the next day to come, so I could get involved with some new girl and promise to marry her and then stop seeing her. In those days, I promised to marry just about every girl I took out. I felt if that's what they wanted to hear, that's what I'd tell them. Maybe it was dishonest, but at the time it didn't seem so.

What the actors had no way of knowing was that the characters were also based on Cassavetes' life. Each of the major characters was a version of himself – in both deep and superficial respects: Tom's tirade about colleges and professors embodied Cassavetes' own attitudes toward higher education. Ben's disenchanted drifting with his two buddies mirrored Cassavetes' own years of street fights, carousing, boozing and skirt-chasing with his two roommates in the early 50s. His love-hate dependency on Hugh was modelled on Cassavetes' rivalry with his elder brother, Nicholas, who was a lot like Hugh and bailed Cassavetes out financially many times in his early years.

Hugh's inability to get a decent job and his feelings about the indignity of the ones that were offered to him echo Cassavetes' own situation before he got his big break. In fact, in 1953 at an audition at the Hudson Theater (a burlesque house), he had had to introduce a girlie line and sing 'A Pretty Girl is Like a Melody' and had been, in his own words, 'humiliated' by the result. A few bars into the song, he was told to shut up and get off the stage.[8]

Hugh also represents a side of Cassavetes from closer to the time that *Shadows* was made. As his career was finally coming together in the mid- and late 50s, Cassavetes felt overwhelmed by requests from friends to help them get jobs or meet important people. Like Hugh, after doing dozens of 'favours' for friends, he would occasionally feel resentful of the demands placed on him and explode with anger and frustration.[9]

Other characters and themes in the film echo Cassavetes' feelings in less specific ways. Rupert's and Hugh's faith in the importance of friendship and Lelia's endearing impulsiveness are reflections of aspects of Cassavetes' personality. Though it was downplayed when the film was re-edited, it is also biographically significant that the first version of *Shadows* focused much more heavily on the idea that Tony 'stole' David's girlfriend from him, which tied in with Cassavetes' personal streak of jealousy and envy in romantic affairs.

More important than these specific references, the idea of 'passing' represented Cassavetes' view of his own situation at this point in his life. As strange as it might sound, Cassavetes thought of himself as being a lot like Lelia and Ben. As the young ethnic actor made his way among New York's artistic movers and shakers in the late 50s, he felt himself to be an impostor in a world he was not part of and was not comfortable within. He felt he was 'passing' for something that was not necessarily a reflection of his truest, deepest identity.

'Buy a ticket to your movie'

One soldier showed up with five dollars after hitchhiking 300 miles to give it to us. And some really weird girl came in off the street; she had a mustache and hair on her legs and the hair on her head was matted with dirt and she wore a filthy polka-dot dress; she was really bad. After walking into the workshop, this girl got down on her knees, grabbed my pants and said, 'You are the Messiah.' I had to look that one up. Anyway, she became our sound editor and soon straightened out her life. In fact, a lot of the people who worked on the film were people who were screwed up – and got straightened out working with the rest of us. From that point on, it didn't matter to me whether or not

Shadows would be any good; it just became a way of life where you got close to people and where you could hear ideas that weren't full of shit.

After the Sunday afternoon improvisation, all Cassavetes and his actors talked about was turning the scene into a movie. Cassavetes had been mulling over the possibility of making a 16mm movie for a number of years. The idea dated back to 1954 or 1955, when Cassavetes had become friends with a German film-maker living in New York named Erich Kollmar. Kollmar had made a documentary in Africa in the early 50s on newly available portable 16mm equipment.[10] When he showed it to Cassavetes, according to Kollmar, the young actor immediately made the imaginative leap and became extremely excited about the possibility of making a feature film this way. Cassavetes discussed the idea with Lane as well, invoking the analogy of off-Broadway theatre: why couldn't there be an off-Broadway *movie*?

But ideas were one thing and raising the money necessary to buy film stock and to rent or buy even minimal lighting and sound-recording equipment was something else. Cassavetes estimated that he would need $7,500 to make a film. Never one to hesitate, he swung into action in his best street-hustler manner. The improv took place on Sunday, 13 January, and two days later Cassavetes contacted the *New York Times* announcing that he was fund-raising for a still untitled 'non-profit' venture dealing with the 'Negro–white problem'. The statement appeared in a brief article on Sunday, 20 January. It was a misrepresentation of what the film was really about, but Cassavetes' crazy dream was that if it seemed like a worthy cause someone might simply write a cheque for the whole amount.

The piece elicited a few responses. There was a smattering of small donations from professional associates – like Cassavetes' agent, Marty Baum, who got the Newborne agency to write a $100 cheque, and Josh Logan, who was directing Gena Rowlands on Broadway, who gave another $100. But all of the bigger offers or inquiries (including one from the NAACP) came with strings attached – from wanting to read the script (which didn't exist) to demanding guarantees of a certain return on the investment. Cassavetes told his assistant, Maurice McEndree, to throw them out.

Cassavetes used the contributions to buy film stock and play around with a camera he borrowed from Shirley Clarke, but he knew he would need a lot more money before he could really do anything. He spent a few more weeks unsuccessfully approaching a few other potential investors, then decided on a new plan of attack. He called the host of an all-night New York radio talk show and asked if he could pay a visit. The host was Jean Shepherd and the show was called *Jean Shepherd's Night People*. Cassavetes had been a guest several times before and the format was tailor-made for someone like him – superficially playful and outrageous, yet slyly serious at the same time. Over the years, Shepherd had gathered a small but enthusiastic following of eccentrics and free-thinkers, whom he referred to as his 'night people', who performed a variety of stunts and pranks at Shepherd's behest. The nominal reason Cassavetes gave for wanting to appear on the show was to thank Shepherd for saying nice things about his performance in the recently released *Edge of the City*. But once he got on the air, he launched into a description of the improvisation that had taken place a few weeks before, described the little bit of filming that had already been done, and said that if only he and his actors had a little more money they could actually make a 'real movie'. The outcome was predictable. Shepherd made an appeal to his listeners. Cassavetes provided the address of his workshop, and Shepherd told everyone listening to 'go down Monday morning and buy an advance ticket for two dollars. A ticket to *your* movie'.[11]

People started streaming in at 10 a.m. on Monday morning and kept coming all week long. One fellow hitchhiked in from Pennsylvania; several others took the bus from New Jersey; the majority streamed in from the five boroughs. Everyone had his or her two dollars in hand and many of them wanted to help work on the film. A number of young actors or actor wannabes showed up looking for jobs. At the end of the week Cassavetes, McEndree and Gilson (whom Cassavetes had appointed the film's producer) had taken in $2,500 in contributions (approximately half from the walk-ins, the other half mailed). The money was important, but of equal importance was the influx of excitement, energy and new blood. Overnight, the workshop had gone from being nearly deserted to being filled with people, humming with activity and talk about 'the movie'. *Shadows* was launched.[12]

Shepherd himself frequently visited the workshop over the next few months. The talk-show host would make three more fund-raising appeals on Cassavetes' behalf over the next two years, keep his listeners updated on the progress of 'their film', and conduct listeners' polls (for example, about who should do the music). Cassavetes made additional fund-raising pitches everywhere he went, including a visit on the *Skitch Henderson and his Orchestra* television programme a few months later.

Meanwhile, with the help of his friend Sam Shaw, who had high-level connections, Cassavetes secured a number of additional contributions in the $100 to $500 range from well-off donors – including Robert Rossen, Sol Siegel, Charles Feldman, José Quintero, Reginald Rose, William Wyler and Hedda Hopper – as well as several further donations from Josh Logan. There was no turning back now. Cassavetes would have to have something to show for their support.

Actors as Technicians

Since Cassavetes hadn't known that his pitch would have such dramatic results, the first month after the money came in was devoted to preparations. Cassavetes got in touch with Kollmar and told him to be ready to start shooting in two weeks. He picked Kollmar not only because he was an experienced cameraman, but because he owned his own 16mm Arriflex and lights. Cassavetes had lots of friends who were professional actors, directors and writers, and he received a lot of advice from them both before and during the shoot. Sydney Poitier sat in on many of the rehearsals. Gregory Ratoff dropped by from time to time. Robert Rossen, who had included a fair amount of 16mm work in his own films, was present throughout the spring of 1957, helping Cassavetes in every way he could. Screenwriter Robert Alan Aurthur, whom Cassavetes had met when working on *Edge of the City* and whom he had hired a few months before to write a television pilot for him to act in, also sat in on the filming of a number of scenes.

But beyond Kollmar's, Rossen's, Aurthur's and the others' somewhat more desultory input, *Shadows* was an amateur production all the way. There was no division of labour and there were no designated duties. The various members of the workshop took turns working on every aspect of the pre-production and production process. The actors provided books, furniture and posters to use for the stage set. Actors like Cliff Carnell, Jay Crecco, and Bob Reeh functioned as technicians, carpenters and grips – working on the crew, then stepping in front of the camera and playing bit parts. Maurice McEndree, who was eventually given both producer and editor credits, illustrates how many different hats any one individual could wear (and how arbitrary the assignment of credits was). He taught classes and managed the day-to-day functioning of the workshop while Cassavetes was busy filming; he dealt with fund-raising, writing letters and making phone calls; he supervised the film's scheduling and budgeting; he built sets; he shot a number of scenes; he acted in several of them (he plays 'Moe-Moe' in the scene in Central Park); and he edited most of the footage when shooting was complete.

Assimilation

After the money and volunteers showed up, but before filming began, Cassavetes sent the actors out to do 'life study'. Hugh Hurd was told to try to find a job. Ben Carruthers, Tom Allen, and Dennis Sallas hung out together in the Times Square area and tried to pick up girls. Though Cassavetes told them that they were doing 'research' on their characters, his real goal was that they would deepen their personal relationships with each other. Cassavetes was convinced that only after Hugh, Ben and Lelia became an off-screen 'family', could they convincingly portray an on-screen one. Goldoni tells how life imitated art at one point during this preparation period, when Hugh had to chase away a boy who came up to them in a restaurant and began harassing her about being out with someone of a different race. She was glad to have her 'big brother' with her to stand up for her.

Cassavetes also provided the actors with brief descriptions of each of the main characters. Most of these notes do not survive, but the following is the text of an actual typed paragraph Cassavetes gave to Ben Carruthers to help him prepare his role.

> Bennie is driven by the uncertainty of his color to beg acceptance in this white man's world. Unlike his brother Hugh or Janet, he has no outlet for his emotions. He has been spending his life trying to decide what color he is. Now that he has chosen the white race as his people, his problem remains acceptance. This is difficult, knowing that he is in a sense betraying his own. His life is an aimless struggle to prove something abstract, his everyday living has no outlet.

The actors also worked out backstories for their characters. For example, in answer to the question of why they were living together, Lelia, Hugh and Ben decided that their parents had died. Lelia Goldoni decided that her character had been 'spoiled rotten' by her brothers so that she 'lived in a very special world' where she had never before had to confront racial realities.

Your Style is Your Budget

Filming was made possible by a number of recent technological innovations. The development by Kodak of Tri-X film (with an ASA of

250) made much of the night-time shooting possible. Kollmar's Arriflex was small enough to carry outside the workshop, but the blimp was so heavy that it was difficult to hand-hold, which is why most of the film was shot on a tripod. Wire-recording technology had recently been replaced by more portable tape-recording techniques. Cassavetes used a quarter-inch RCA crystal synch tape deck.[13] Kollmar and Crecco, who ran the deck, came up with a number of ingenious ways to record the sound (which was, needless to say, confined to a single track). Depending on the situation, they used either a Telefunkin 'pencil mike' or a lavaliere 'lapel mike'. In group scenes where the actors were standing still, they hung the Telefunkin from the ceiling. In scenes like the post-party moment where Hugh, Rupert and their girlfriends talk, they put the microphone on the table, just outside the frame. In scenes that involved movement, they had the actor with the softest voice in a group wear the lavaliere with the wire snaked inside his clothing. (Among the siblings, Ben Carruthers was the one who most frequently wore it, since he was given to mumbling under his breath, much to the annoyance of Kollmar and Crecco. Kollmar said that there are so many close-ups of him because they could position the mike closer to his face that way.)[14]

Sam Shaw, who had worked in the New York film scene for many years, talked Spyros Skouras, the owner of Delux Film Labs, into contributing film stock and letting Cassavetes use the lab for processing, where Otto Paoloni, one of the finest technicians in the world, provided occasional advice on salvaging some of the more poorly lit footage. However, there was more than enough amateurism to counteract Paoloni's expertise.

To make things more chaotic than they already were, consonant with Cassavetes' belief that it was important to involve as many people as possible in the production and his feeling that 'how you shoot a film is a diversion', Cassavetes encouraged everyone to take turns operating the camera when Kollmar wasn't around. McEndree remembers filming the bedroom scene between Lelia and Tony as well as the scene in the Museum of Modern Art sculpture garden. Cliff Carnell, Seymour Cassel, and other actors and crew members shot other scenes. Cassavetes, who at that point knew almost nothing about photography, shot some himself. The result was variations in exposure or focus even within a single sequence. For example, the scene of Lelia and Tony walking along the pavement was shot from two different angles by two different operators. Whoever shot the straight-ahead shots and the close-up inserts of Tony's face took care to focus the camera sharply. Whoever filmed the countershot close-ups of Lelia in a separate set-up across the street with a telephoto lens, seriously misjudged the focus.

On the other side of the equation, in such an amateur production, virtuosity could be almost as bad as ineptness. Cassavetes persuaded Robert Rossen to light and shoot several scenes, including the nightclub scene where Hugh sings and introduces the chorus line. But in Cassavetes' opinion, Rossen's three-point lighting and polished photography turned out so beautifully that it made the rest of the film look bad.

Fake Locations
Cassavetes milked the 'shot on the streets of New York' rubric for all it was worth in the film's press coverage, giving the impression that filming was a cat-and-mouse game between his merry gang of pranksters and the police. However, the facts were that he avoided shooting on the streets as much as he possibly could.

The workshop stage with a slighly different set. Burt Lane is on the right. Workshop students comprise the audience (Courtesy Burt Lane)

The main set for the film was built on the Variety Arts stage by McEndree and a few of the actors. The stage (which can be recognised by its large columns, exposed pipes, high back windows, and brick back wall with peeling paint) was used for all of the scenes in the livingroom and dining room of the Carruthers' apartment as well as for the scene in which Lelia dances with Davey Jones. Several other sets for scenes which did not make it into the final edit were also built on the Variety Arts stage: another livingroom set; a bedroom set; a set made to look like a corner table in a coffee shop.

Dave Simon, who had been an electrician before he decided to become an actor, ingeniously rigged rudimentary lighting over the workshop stage by covering the ceiling with aluminium foil and stringing 150-watt bulbs every few feet. The lighting scheme unfortunately backfired, proving to be too bright, flat and 'filled', and creating a washed-out look in many of the shots in the siblings' apartment. It was too overexposed for even Paoloni to correct.[15] It didn't help that Kollmar's light meter was left in a bar early in the film-making process, so that he had to eyeball his exposures after that.

The 'rock-and-roll party' that appears under the credits was created in one of the small rooms off to one side of main stage space. As an indication of how Cassavetes employed psychology to motivate his actors and crews, he deliberately included as many people from the workshop as possible in the scene to build morale. The entire acting group crammed themselves into a 7 x 10-ft. storage room, Cassavetes positioned the cameraman on a ladder against one wall, and simply told Ben to 'find a way to get to the back corner'.

Many other scenes were shot in cordoned-off indoor locations. The rehearsal hall sequence was shot in an actual rehearsal hall on 8th Avenue near 48th Street. The nightclub scene was shot in a real basement nightclub, the Bal Tamborin, where Tom Allen worked as a comedian and obtained permission for Cassavetes to use.

'Cheese it, the cops!'

One day we were shooting in an alley … We were shooting a fight scene. We had permission from all the people around the neighborhood to allow us to shoot in this alley, and we were shooting this fight, and a police car pulled up and one of the cops came out and shot a gun in the air, and one of our actors fainted dead away![16]

Since the street shots presented the greatest challenge, Cassavetes held them to an absolute minimum, shot virtually all of them within two blocks of the workshop, and 'faked' many of them (by placing the camera inside a restaurant or store and photographing through the plate-glass window). Since he and his crew didn't have permits to block off pavements or streets (because they couldn't afford the insurance the City of New York required as a precondition), and since they sometimes had to run cables across the lines of a crosswalk, or position the camera in a location where it caused rubbernecking and traffic slow-downs, police were instructed to disperse the group. The first line of defence, according to Burt Lane, was to plead that it was 'a student movie', and that permits weren't necessary. That only worked for the first few days. The next tactic was to offer a nominal bribe. According to Sam Shaw, to get the final shots of the cars coming at the camera and Bennie crossing through traffic at night on 8th Avenue near 48th Street, Cassavetes paid off a policeman from the 47th precinct. Lelia Goldoni reports that during the scene in which she and Tony walk together, several palmed ten-spots bought respite from the police, until more of the city's finest came along requesting their fair share and Cassavetes' money ran out. In Cassavetes' version of a contemporary three-card monte operation, he would also post lookouts so that the production could pack up and make a rapid getaway to a less conspicuous location when necessary. It helped that one of the actors was a part-time cab driver who would park his cab next to wherever they were shooting so that they could throw the camera into it and go.

As far as lighting went, necessity was the mother of invention. Cassavetes had David Simon mount two automobile headlights on two-by-fours to make a portable light source that could be powered from any available automobile battery (especially if the vehicle's owner wasn't in sight – it was the era before hood locks). Lelia Goldoni said that Cassavetes used this contraption to 'fill' during the scene in which she and Tony walk and talk, and Burt Lane says that although the new faster film stocks allowed for almost all of the night scenes to be shot in existing light, Cassavetes used the headlight rig to key the fight scene.

The tendency of the outdoor shooting to draw crowds of onlookers is why, as much as possible, it was done at night or with the camera positioned in a somewhat concealed or off-street location. Cassavetes put a lot of thought into finding outdoor locations that would not draw attention (unintentionally ending up with some quite original angles and backgrounds). As illustrations: the fight scene was originally supposed to take place in the courtyard of an apartment complex, which itself is an off-street location, but when some of the residents complained about the noise, it was moved 'indoors' to the dumpster that appears in the film. Similarly, when Ben is shown going down into the basement club following his recitation of 'Mary had a little lamb', the standard way to photograph the scene would be to show him going into the club from street level, but to avoid being seen, the camera was positioned in the stairwell. For the same reason, many of the apparent outdoors scenes were actually photographed from indoors or from within a doorway (in one shot, the doorway of the Variety Arts building) looking out onto the street. Many of the early shots of Ben on the street were done this way.

Telephoto lenses were used both in shots made from indoors looking out and in shots actually filmed outdoors to keep the camera, and the attention it drew, away from the actors. To get the final shot of Ben walking off into the night, the camera was placed on the rooftop of Roseland. Hugh's runs through the bus station were similarly filmed from high on the main stairway so that none of the people down on the concourse realised that he or she was in a movie or that Hugh was anything more than a harried commuter late for his train. A telephoto lens was used in other scenes (like the Central Park scene and the scene involving Tony and Lelia on the pavement) first because Cassavetes did not have the money to rent tracks to follow the characters, and second so that he could keep the camera far enough away so that gawkers would not be in the shot. It's worth noting that although 70s movies accustomed audiences to the use of telephoto lens photography, contemporary viewers found the shots in which Lelia and Tony walk toward the camera on the pavement visually shocking. The scene was characterised by many reviewers as bizarre and disorientating, since the characters were walking toward the camera, yet apparently not getting any closer.

A Party Atmosphere
Filming began around the beginning of March 1957 and continued on an irregular basis until the middle of May. The crew, indoors or out, seldom exceeded five or six people: Cassavetes, Kollmar, Crecco (sound), Simon (lighting), McEndree and Carnell (grips). Counting the actors, the total was fewer than a dozen people present at one time for all but the party scenes. Cassavetes felt that the small size was not a drawback but an advantage since it kept everyone personally involved and energised.

The atmosphere was entirely different from a studio shoot. Everyone was friends with everyone else, and there was lots of laughing, talking and kibitzing (not to mention a little drunken partying on occasion). Cassavetes was a night person at heart and scheduled most of the filming for the evenings, particularly for scenes shot in the Variety Arts stage or building (since that was the time the stage space was free, the actors were most available and the stage space was quietest). Because the shoots sometimes ran all night long, it was not uncommon for Cassavetes and whoever was still around at dawn to go out and eat breakfast together at the Howard Johnson's on Broadway and 49th, or at the all-night Horn & Hardart Automat on 42nd between 7th and 8th. Other mornings, Sam Shaw would invite Cassavetes back to his house, where his wife, Anne, would make breakfast for the two men.

Improvisation Within Given Circumstances

Since it was my first film, I thought everything had to be painstakingly planned: 'Go here. There. Do it again. Again, again, again!' I was a maniac because I was so scared of making a mistake. After the second, third and fourth films I didn't need to plan the shots anymore because making a movie wasn't so frightening for me.

Cliff Carnell (who acted and worked on the crew), Erich Kollmar and Cassavetes shooting with Kollmar's 16mm Arriflex (© Sam Shaw)

Although Cassavetes attempted to cash in on the post-Beat fascination with 'improvisation', and cultivated the impression in interviews that the actors had more or less winged the movie, the facts were quite different. It was true that the actors came up with most of the specific words they spoke in the initial period of shooting, but their inventions were severely limited by conditions that Cassavetes laid down. From that very first Sunday afternoon improvisation, Cassavetes stipulated the personalities of the characters, their relationships, the events and usually the dramatic outcome of each scene. Though some of the events might change during the course of filming a scene, the actors were never really on their own. Prior to each day's shooting, Cassavetes and McEndree would sit down and work out the next day's scenes in some detail. The actors' improvisations were always staged within specific 'given circumstances'.

A second level of control and shaping came during the actual filming process. Cassavetes didn't hesitate to give directions or to work toward a pre-decided outcome. In the key scene, for example, Hugh Hurd reported that Cassavetes 'definitely wanted a reconciliation' to take place, and kept shooting over and over again until he got what he wanted: 'There were lots of takes with fighting, lots that didn't go the way John wanted, but they

Cassavetes directing Hugh and Rupert on the workshop stage in the scene in which they interrupt Lelia and Tony (© Sam Shaw)

31

didn't show up in the film.' Every actor I have spoken with confirmed that when Cassavetes was determined to capture a certain kind of moment on film, he was relentless in his pursuit of it and extremely hard to please. As an illustration, Cassavetes shot a seduction scene where Lelia and Tony kissed more than fifty times – until Goldoni's lips were swollen and bleeding from the effects of Tony's repeated kisses – and was still not satisfied with the result. He wanted to continue and was only prevented by Goldoni's protests that she just couldn't go on. None of these takes was used in the final print. As Erich Kollmar told me, 'Sometimes the original ideas were the actors'; sometimes they were John's; but after the hours of rehearsing it, John would get what he wanted. In any case, he would be the one to recognise it, to decide if it was right or not.'

'A lot was written down'

> I thought it was funny when critics took the improvisation thing too seriously. It was a joke. I don't think the ultimate effect of the film has anything to do with improvisation. That's only a method. The reason *Shadows* was done that way was that I didn't think I'd be able to write a script, and I couldn't afford to hire a screenwriter. So I explained the general ideas to the actors. If we had had a writer, we would have used a script. There was no script, but there was an outline. We stuck to it very carefully. We would work on the idea of each scene before we would shoot it. It was just like revising a script, except that there were no written words – we kept the idea and the script in our minds. We started out with just a couple of typewritten pages of background, but as we went along a lot was written down about the characters.

Cassavetes lived to regret the title card placed at the end of the film, since it dogged the rest of his career. He later stated that if he had had confidence in his own ability to write a script before he began and had had time to do it after the money and the volunteers showed up, he would have, and the film would not have been any different.

'Stylistic unity drains the humanity out of a text'

> If the film is primarily the creation of the director or the writer, then you have only a single viewpoint upon the theme. It is the creation of only one imagination. But if the film is created out of the actors, then the work has as many facets as there are actors; the action is seen in the

round – the communal creation of *several* imaginations. Consider the movie as artwork on canvas. You begin with ideas, something of your own, somebody else adds something different and it changes a bit. Stylistic unity drains the humanity out of a text.

There was a doubleness in Cassavetes' method, however. Even as he reigned the actors in and had very strong ideas about what he wanted from them, he insisted that they should bring a lot of themselves and their own ideas to the role. In fact, in Cassavetes' view, the difference between *Shadows* and most other films resided almost entirely in the centrality of the actor's contribution to the creative process. The goal of most directors, particularly virtuosic ones like Sternberg, Welles, Hitchcock and Kubrick, is to impose *their* vision on their works, so that each shot, scene and interaction bears *their* imprint. Cassavetes went in the opposite direction, depending heavily on his *performers'* input. If the first kind of film-making can be called 'concentrative' – so that the points of view of the various figures within the work ultimately cumulate in a single, overarching way of seeing and feeling, Cassavetes' might be called 'dispersive', because it imagines the work to be the product of as many different personal voices, styles and moods as possible. The point was not to unify the work around a singular point of view, but to diversify it by allowing in as many different points of view as possible.

Loose Lips Sink Ships
Actors developed their characters separately, and, if necessary, kept secrets from each other about what their characters felt, wanted, or knew. The danger was that if actors discussed their roles with each other, they might unconsciously incorporate each other's views into their own, homogenise the work, and play their relationship falsely. It represented another difference of opinion with Strasberg:

> I differ from the working method advocated by Stanislavski and followed by the Actors Studio, which involves group discussion of the characters. For me each role must be an individual's conception as well as an individual creation. If each role is the result of communal study by director and ensemble, everything will dovetail; it will all be nice and neat and smooth; but the conflict of the characters won't be truthful. The actors don't discuss their interpretations sitting around in a group. The general theme of the work, of course, must be studied by the whole group, so that we share the same overall conception; but each actor must

come at his own interpretation of his role, without the sort of group study and mutual criticism which one associates with Method work.

Creating Differences

Cassavetes' interest in differences of feeling and point of view was such an important part of the creative process that, when necessary, he would deliberately foment disagreements and misunderstandings between actors to create on-screen drama. He frequently pitted actors against each other, gave them conflicting directions just prior to filming a scene, or put them in slightly different emotional moods – even if he had to deceive them to do it.

Two illustrations will suffice to make the point. The first example is connected with the reshoot of the film which used a script: in the scene in which Tony walks Lelia back to his apartment, Cassavetes told Lelia that he couldn't give her her lines until the morning of the shoot because he was still writing the scene up until the last minute. It was a lie. The scene had been finished and Tony had been given his lines a week earlier. The result was to create a deliberately unbalanced dramatic situation. Tony's performance is poised and confident; Lelia's is tentative and hesitant. Tony dominates the interaction, takes the lead tonally, and even completes some of Lelia's sentences for her (when she forgets her lines).

Cassavetes employed a similar tactic in the scene in which Ben returns with the apartment keys following his fight with Hugh. Cassavetes privately gave contradictory directions to each actor. He took Ben Carruthers aside and told him the point of the scene was for him to go in, throw the keys down, and get out as quickly as possible. What he didn't tell Ben was that he had previously told Hugh Hurd that the point of the scene was for the two brothers to make up, and that Hugh should use the moment to heal the rift between him and his younger brother.

Playing with Actors' Feelings

Both moments illustrate Cassavetes' characteristic directorial manner. Rather than giving actions or blocking, he would manipulate the actors' emotions (usually putting them in slightly different emotional states). As he once put it, he didn't 'direct' so much as 'set up situations'. The result was that the actor couldn't always tell where a scene was going. There was an open-ended unpredictability to the dramatic event. His goal was to get the actors to a place where they were genuinely responding to each other. In the key scene, Ben and Hugh weren't really sure what the other would do next or exactly how it would all come out. Even if an actor knew how a scene was supposed to end, the path it took to get there each time could be slightly different and fairly surprising.

Cassavetes didn't hesitate to be manipulative when he thought it might improve a scene. In *Faces*, he climbed under a table and tickled Lynn Carlin to get her to laugh during the supper table conversation. Burt Lane remembers Cassavetes pinching an actress's bottom to get a startled look on her face. When Lelia Goldoni was having trouble expressing affection during the kissing scene with Tony, Cassavetes called a break and whispered to Sam Shaw that he should send Tony on an errand and ask Ben (who was Lelia's boyfriend and worked on the crew during most of her scenes) to man the camera in order to get an affectionate look on her face.

Deviousness was not out of the question. Prior to filming the Grand Central scene in which Rupert erupts in a paroxysm of frustration and anger, Cassavetes coldly and calculatedly repeated a racist remark the Station Master had uttered that made Rupert *really* upset. Hugh said that much of the emotional intensity of Rupert's speech about leaving the country – 'I've had it! I've been insulted by these pigs, laughed at … Let's get out of here. We'll go to Paris, France, Africa … I don't care!'[17] was attributable to the fact that Rupert was expressing his *real* emotions at the moment. As his friend and fellow actor, Hugh had to '*really* calm him down' and 'hold him in the scene' – to quote Hurd's description of the

Counter-directions forced the actors to stay in the moment, genuinely responsive and open, just as the characters are asked to be

36   The 'Night to Remember' sequence: Hugh really had to calm Rupert down and 'hold him in the scene'

moment. At this point of authenticity, life and art become indistinguishable. The scene is no longer 'pretend'. The actors Hugh Hurd and Rupert Crosse were really experiencing what the characters Hugh and Rupert were living.

Where reality and acting overlap in this way, the actors must remain genuinely responsive to each other's feelings and expressions. A scene is not about saying lines, but grappling with real emotions. The result is the characteristic step-by-step quality of Cassavetes' scenic presentation – a series of moves and countermoves, where the subject of the scene is not the end point, but the process of getting there.

Developing Emotions on Film
Cassavetes reversed the normal shooting practice in which scenes are broken up into a large number of brief moments. He exposed an entire 400-ft. magazine load (11 minutes of film) for almost every scene he filmed, frequently shooting more than one magazine since a scene might require filming more than once. The point was to allow the actors' emotions to develop in real time. Though the method may have originated to compensate for the absence of a shooting script, in order to allow the actors to feel out their relationships and work out their lines, it worked so well that Cassavetes employed it in all of his subsequent films.[18]

Real and Reel Life
Though Cassavetes romanticised the making of the film when he talked about it, in fact there were a number of serious problems before, during and after the shoot. The struggles and fights he had with various members of the cast and crew incidentally indicate how much control he exerted over every aspect of the shoot.

As the reference to Janet in the note for Ben Carruthers indicates, the 'Lelia' part was originally intended for another member of the workshop, Janet Conway, who dropped out when her actor-boyfriend, Tom Gilson was thrown off the production. According to Maurice McEndree, who was Gilson's roommate at the time:

> Just before we were to begin filming, Tom Gilson and his girlfriend Janet, who were to be the leads, and Burt Lane, who was to be producer, formed an alliance and gave John an ultimatum to do it their way or they would walk. John came up to me the next morning, while I was preparing the studio apartment set and said 'Do you want to be the producer?' I asked: 'Who's going to play the parts?' 'Tony and Lelia', John replied.

Prior to that, Tony Ray was the assistant director and Lelia Goldoni was working as his assistant.

Cassavetes had many struggles with Erich Kollmar. As the one experienced 'professional' on the film, Kollmar was never comfortable either with the improvised nature of the production or with Cassavetes' apparent indifference to technical concerns. Kollmar wanted rehearsals. He wanted to block actors' movements and establish 'marks' for them to hit so he could light shots properly. He cared intensely about the photography and wanted it to look as good as possible. Cassavetes was opposed to rehearsals, since he thought they dampened spontaneity, and he wanted to shoot scenes as much as possible using fill lighting and master-shot set-ups to allow the actors to move freely and naturally and to keep the camera away from them. Kollmar argued with him frequently and almost quit more than once. Since he was one of the few essential members of the production, Cassavetes persuaded him to stay on by making a series of promises. He told him he would give him equal billing to his own in the credits, talk up his work with producers, and help him get a studio directing job (promising to commit himself to act in the first film Kollmar directed). Once shooting was complete and Cassavetes had gotten everything he needed from Kollmar, he reneged on all of his promises (even the size of Kollmar's credit, which would have cost Cassavetes nothing). Kollmar to this day is bitter about how Cassavetes 'used' him.

Cassavetes was liberal with promises. When Burt Lane had problems with the appropriation of the workshop stage and spaces for moviemaking, Cassavetes assured him that *Shadows* was only a preliminary project and that he and Lane would be working on four or five more films together that would put them and the workshop on a sound financial basis. When *Shadows* was finished, that vow also was forgotten. There were a number of problems with actors during and after the shoot. Lelia Goldoni, who was personally fond of Cassavetes and worked with him again in *Johnny Staccato*, was exasperated by his treatment of her in several scenes. Hugh Hurd, who also liked Cassavetes and worked with him again in *A Woman Under the Influence*, was extremely angry with Cassavetes on many occasions and argued with him about cutting what Hurd felt was his 'biggest and best scene'.[19]

Cassavetes' clashes with David Pokotilow were even more heated. Pokotilow was not an actor but a concert violinist (later playing with the Pittsburgh Symphony). After appearing in a few scenes, he lost interest and didn't show up for the Central Park scene. Cassavetes lied to him as well to persuade him to continue. He told him his scenes were essential because he was the romantic lead, the film's hero. When Pokotilow saw the final movie, he felt he had been made a fool of.

The struggles were discouraging for Cassavetes. He describes the final day of filming:

> In the course of the filming, the tide of outside enthusiasm dwindled and finally turned into rejection. The *Shadows* people continued, no longer with the hope of injecting the industry with vitality, but only for the sake of their pride in themselves and in the film that they were all devoted to. On the last day of shooting, I couldn't turn on the camera. I was so fed up with doing it because there was no love of the craft or the idea or anything. We're doing this experiment, and now it's the last day, nobody's here except McEndree and me. He couldn't turn on the camera and I couldn't turn on the camera and Ben was standing there asking, 'Are you going to roll this thing or not?' We're just standing there looking at each other. We couldn't turn on this camera because it had been such a hassle.

'We made every mistake known to man'

It would be almost eighteen months after the end of shooting before Cassavetes would have a screenable print. A number of problems immediately became apparent. The sound was no sooner processed than Cassavetes discovered that most of it was unusable. Many of the voices were too faint to be heard, and many scenes were punctuated with extraneous background noises, like the sounds of doors slamming or dancers practising. Re-recording the dialogue was complicated by the fact that no one had thought to keep a record of what the actors had said. Cassavetes had to take the film to a school for lip-readers and get stenographers to transcribe what the actors had said, then bring the actors back for looping sessions.[20]

There were many other problems. Many shots didn't match. Actors showed up on different days wearing different clothing. Ben wore three different sweaters underneath his black leather jacket, forgetting that the jacket would be unzipped in some shots and show the difference. Some days he wore white gloves, other days black gloves, and other days no gloves in shots that ended up being edited together. The editing challenge was compounded by the fact that almost no thought had been given to shooting basic cut-away coverage or transitional footage. The final problem was the sheer amount of film that had to be gone through.

In his two months of shooting, Cassavetes had shot more than 60,000 ft., or roughly thirty hours, for what would eventually become a 60-minute movie. Given the number of mistakes he had made, it is not entirely surprising that he spent more than $15,000 (the equivalent in contemporary dollars of around $150,000), twice what he had thought the film would cost when he began.

In November 1958, Cassavetes put the word out to Shepherd, and Shepherd announced to his listeners that there would be three free midnight screenings at the Paris Theater. McEndree had scrupulously kept a list of the names and addresses of all of the contributors and made sure they were also invited and admitted. It should have been the end of the story, but Cassavetes' problems were only beginning.

'People started to leave and I began perspiring'

I went to a theater-owner friend of mine and I said, 'Look, we want to show our film and we can fill this theater.' It was the Paris Theater in New York and 600 people filled that theater and we turned away another 400 people at the door. About 15 minutes into the film the people started to leave. And they left. And they left! And I began

Shafi Hadi was one of eight musicians who performed with Mingus initially. He added solos in a second session (© Sam Shaw)

perspiring and the cast was getting angry...We all sat closer and closer together and pretty soon there wasn't anyone in the theater!

Cassavetes exaggerates on several counts. First, the screenings were not mobbed. Only about 100 people showed up for any of them. Many of the seats were empty. Second, everyone did not leave before the end. Only a large number of them. But, in every other respect, the screening could not have gone worse. To start with, the sound was so bad that McEndree and Cassavetes had to keep running back to the projection booth to try to improve it. Even more importantly, with only one or two exceptions, even the viewers who stayed until the end to participate in a question and answer session told Cassavetes they didn't like the movie. They found the story incoherent, hard to understand, and 'arty'.

'Falling in love with stylistic effects'

> I was an actor who had gotten behind the camera and decided to be like all people on their first film – that this is magic and a magical instrument and I was going to use it marvelously and shoot just *impressions* of what people said and *impressions* of what people were, rather than shooting inside the people.

The main objections most of the viewers expressed were that they couldn't tell what was going on and couldn't follow the story. They said the film felt more like a series of disjointed episodes than a narrative story. In reply, Cassavetes said he had, in fact, put storytelling in second place behind the attempt to craft a 'mood piece' that captured the feelings of the characters in a series of poetic visual effects.

Since that print, and not the current version of *Shadows*, is Cassavetes' real 'first film', it would be fascinating to view it now. Unfortunately, Cassavetes cut up the negative to make the second version and none of the original prints survive.[21] However, since approximately half an hour of the version screened that night was included in the print that comes down to us, present-day viewers can get a pretty good idea of what the original film looked like by thinking of an entire movie constituted of 'atmosphere' moments like the following ones, which survive in the current edit. Each of these scenes has a distinctive visual 'look' and represents an attempt to capture a certain 'mood' or 'feeling'.

- The rock and roll party that now begins the film but originally occurred in the middle of it.
- The daytime sequences early in the movie in which Ben walks down the street.
- Hugh's two sprints through Grand Central Station.
- The sequence in which Tony, Lelia and David walk through Central Park, followed by the moment in which Tony and Lelia run across the lawn, over a wall, under the trees and through traffic.
- The brief laughter and staring montages just prior to the fight scene at Hugh's party.
- The final fight sequence and the night-time scenes that follow.

Extrapolate a 60-minute feature from these 'poetic' moments and you have the film that the initial viewers saw. The first version of *Shadows* was much more consistently a *visual* experience. In fact, one way of detecting early footage that still remains in the film is to look for various forms of visual virtuosity. One of Cassavetes' favourite techniques was to shoot *through* or *past* something in the foreground. He composed many shots with something visible between the camera and the characters. In the apartment set, he shot through a rope latticework and past a bottle on a table and the ceiling fixture over the table. In the Central Park scene, he shot through or past trees, rocks and fences. In some of the telephoto shots of the street (whether they actually were shot on the street or through a plate-glass window), he enjoys having cars and passers-by come between the camera and the characters. Another striking visual technique Cassavetes employed was to use tilts and raking angles from below, as in the shots of Lelia's and Tony's flight from David, or from above, as in the shot of Ben near the end of the movie. A final technique was to use shots that were simply visually striking or unusual. The final two minutes are a showcase of such visually dazzling moments: from the shots of the headlights coming directly at the camera when Ben crosses the street, to the reflections of store lights off the car hoods, to the play of the neon lights on Ben as he walks away at the end.

Starting Over
Cassavetes had invited a representative from British Lion to the screenings. He broke the news to the film-maker that the film was not releasable in its present form and gave Cassavetes a list of suggested changes. Beyond the incoherence of the story, he had objections to three specific scenes. In the rehearsal hall and nightclub sequences, Cassavetes had used an Irving Berlin song, 'A Pretty Girl is Like a Melody', which he didn't have the

rights to; in Tony's post-coital conversation with Lelia, Tony used the word 'virgin'; and in the fight scene, one of the boys said 'Fuck you' and a 'Fuck you' graffito was prominently visible in the background.

Nicos Papadakis, a European producer who happened to be present, reassured Cassavetes that the film could be saved if only 'a few narrative holes were filled in'. The problem was that at a drunken party a few nights before the Paris Theater screenings, Cassavetes and McEndree had thrown everything they had not used down the incinerator chute. Any footage to be added would have to be filmed afresh. It was a discouraging realisation. Cassavetes faced the prospect of devoting a third year of his life to a project he was beginning to feel might never end.

The British Lion representative offered to put up $5,000 for the reshoot. Papadakis told Cassavetes he could raise a few thousand dollars more. In reward he was given a tiny part as Lelia's masher in the Times Square movie theatre scene. Cassavetes was promised $10,000 from two other investors (though only a small part of the money ever materialised). He thought that was enough to do it.

Cassavetes contacted good friend Robert Alan Aurthur and went over the print with him, shot by shot, scene by scene. The goal was to use as much of the old negative as they could, then reassemble the original cast and add a series of scenes that would clarify the narrative and enlarge some of the characters' parts. There would be no time for improvisation now, since Cassavetes wanted to squeeze the entire reshoot into a two-week period. It was important to have a finished script in hand to give to the actors before they showed up. Cassavetes and Aurthur wrote more than an hour of new scenes. Cassavetes called up the major members of the cast and crew, who had dispersed to points as far away as Los Angeles, and made arrangements for them to come back to New York. It was now two years after the first version had been shot, and persuading them to re-gather was not easy. To entice them, Cassavetes deceptively told them that he had a distribution deal that would make them rich and famous if only they would agree to be in a few more scenes. It was a lie, and would be the source of misunderstandings, complaints and an eventual lawsuit; but Cassavetes was willing to do whatever was necessary to make it happen. The reshoot was scheduled for February or March 1959.[22]

The Second Version

The second version was much deeper. I think the greatest things in the film, I mean the best things in the film, were shot in the reshooting, in a ten-day period. Which has to tell you something, because it took us four months to shoot the [improvised] version.[23]

The Appendix lists the scenes added in the reshoot. Cassavetes and Aurthur were quite ingenious in their patchwork, which is why in almost fifty years no one has noticed it. Since the main goal was to make the narrative seem less disjointed, one technique they employed was to have most of the new scenes allude to a following scene. They introduced a scene between Lelia and Hugh in the train station that not only motivated his mad dash through the station, but introduced her walk past the movie theatres and her desire to be independent. They added the joke-telling scene to serve as a transition into the nightclub scene and to enlarge the theme of Hugh being insulted and his feelings being hurt. The Fountain scene mentions the visit to the Museum of Modern Art that follows it and the literary party at David's in the scene following that one. They added the scene in the cab to function as a transitional device to get Lelia and Tony from Tony's apartment back to hers. The conversation they added between Hugh and Lelia in the bedroom mentions Hugh's party that follows it.

The dovetailing was far from perfect, however. Even beyond the technical differences between the old and new footage (both the sound

44   Cassavetes as Lelia's protector and Nicos Papadakis as the masher. Both versions are marked by busy backgrounds and filled frames

recording and the image quality are appreciably better in the reshoot), the two sets of scenes failed to match in dozens of ways. Since they were filmed two years apart, most of the younger actors look distinguishably more youthful in the original scenes. On top of all of that, virtually no one is wearing exactly the same clothing in the two shoots – even Hugh's white cap is slightly different in the later shoot. The Appendix has a complete breakdown of more than a hundred changes in characters' appearances. It is evidence of how tolerant an audience is of such discrepancies that these differences not only don't disrupt the viewing experience, but have never even been noticed.

Covering Their Tracks

Cassavetes and Aurthur worked around a number of logistical obstacles and constraints. Since the stage set originally used for the Carruthers apartment had been destroyed after the first version was filmed and there was no time to build new sets on the Variety Arts stage (and there was still some bad blood between Lane and Cassavetes over the earlier shoot), Cassavetes used the apartment he and Rowlands shared on 75th between Fifth and Madison as the location for many of the new scenes. The livingroom became the set for David's literary party. A bedroom became the room where Sam, Rupert and Hugh practise telling jokes. Another bedroom became the two Carruthers' bedrooms. A few of the film's sharp-eyed early reviewers noticed the glaring mismatch of the siblings' orange-crate livingroom furniture and their maple bedroom set.

Another problem Cassavetes surmounted was his inability to secure the use of the basement club where the nightclub scene had been filmed. The first version had an argument between Hugh, Rupert and Ackerman in the dressing-room that Cassavetes wanted to greatly enlarge. When he found out that he couldn't film in the club, he re-wrote the old rehearsal hall scene and created the completely new joke-telling scene to bring the same thematic elements into the film.

The three specific issues that British Lion raised were dealt with. Tony would be told to say 'If I'd known it was the first time …' The offending shots in the fight scene were omitted (though a scrawled 'Fuck you' is still faintly visible in the background of several shots). A new song written by Jack Ackerman, who played the impresario and was an actual songwriter (he would write the music for *Faces* and *The Killing of a Chinese Bookie*), was looped into both the rehearsal hall and the nightclub sequences. Since there was no money to clear rights, when he re-edited

Shadows Cassavetes cleverly recycled two other songs Ackerman had written for the first version. When he was stuck for a song for Davey and Lelia to dance to in the reshoot, he used Ackerman's 'Beautiful', which Tony and Lelia had danced to, a second time.[24] The music emanating from the club Ben descends into, was also recycled for the sequence under the credits.

Despite his later claims that he had used direct sound throughout, Cassavetes extensively used looping to cover changes and inconsistencies between the two versions. A conservative estimate would be that between a third and a half of the present film contains dialogue added in the studio.

Stylistic Razzle-dazzle

Cassavetes claimed that he had learned his lesson about creating striking visual effects, but it is revealing that the later footage is as visually precious as the earlier. The face-off between Ben and the 'mask' in the sculpture garden or the use of the 'Night to Remember' background in Hugh and Rupert's train station conversation is as arty as anything in the

46   A film of breakdowns: characters' smiling public faces suddenly reveal pain or shame. Hugh's pretence of calm and control disappear

earlier version. The scene of Lelia walking past movie theatres and
looking at the posters features the same busy backgrounds that the shot of
Tony making the phone call did. The 'Charge' scene, the rehearsal hall
scene, the joke-telling scene, the post-coital scene, and the scene in Lelia's
bedroom are as fond of tight-figured two-, three- and four-shots as the
argument scene preceding the final fight in the first version (and as
indebted to John Huston). The shooting past foreground and
middleground objects in the refilmed sections of the rehearsal hall scene
is no different from the use of intervening objects in the first version (and
as indebted to Sternberg). Cassavetes equally abhors empty frame space
in both versions, filling the frame in any way he can – with objects and
people in front of or behind the main characters or with the faces or
bodies of supporting characters. There are also a number of 'bravura'
tracking movements in the reshoot. Cassavetes didn't have a dolly when
he made the first version, but rented one for the reshoot of the rehearsal
hall scene and the final train station scene between Rupert and Hugh.
Particularly in the rehearsal hall sequence, many of the tracking
movements are as gratuitous as the static visual effects in the first version.

Cassavetes employed many self-consciously 'artistic' effects – from close-figured three- and
four-shots, to the mask images, to Ben's 'Mary had a little lamb'

In short, Cassavetes the director is still a boy with a toy, not entirely over his infatuation with stylistic razzle-dazzle.[25]

Cinematic Impressionism
Although critics called Cassavetes a 'realist', he thought of himself as an 'impressionist'. His point was that he was not concerned with the outsides but the insides of experience, and was less interested in telling a story, than in presenting a succession of shifting feelings. Just as a painting that may appear to be a smooth, seamless representation at a distance resolves itself into a series of irregular, separate brush strokes when it is looked at more closely, at first viewing Cassavetes' scenes may appear to be sequential and continuous, but upon closer inspection they break up into a series of emotional pulse beats. The scene involving Sam, Hugh and Rupert in Sam's room or Ben, Tom and Dennis in the Museum of Modern Art sculpture garden illustrates the effect. Each is less a continuous narrative than a kaleidoscopic succession of shifting feelings and interactions. Characters argue with each other, make up, laugh together, flare out in anger, tease each other, and so on in a seemingly unending series of interactions and solo riffs. The scenes are less documentary records of what conversations really sound like than they are efforts to present as many shifting feelings, moods and alliances as possible. No mood lasts for more than a few seconds. Every relationship keeps changing. It's all tonal jumps and jitterbug jukes. Experience does not progress in a straight line like a plot, but zigzags through a series of changing emotional positions and counterpositions, thrusts and parries, approaches and withdrawals, bits and pieces of this and that.

In this respect, the second version of the film is less a repudiation of the sensibility of the first than a refinement of it. In the first version, Cassavetes attempted to depict a series of emotional pulse beats through 'poetic' shots of characters moving through the cityscape. In the second version, he does it with the characters' interactions. The pulse beats of emotion just come faster and more fluidly in the second version – because they come with every change of tone in a character's voice. But early or late, the goal was the same: to present a world of oil where nothing stands still.

Rock Around the Clock
The reshooting went on at a frantic pace for fourteen days and, as was the case with the 1957 shoot, was not done in sequence. Locations were used

whenever they became available, which often led to 24/7 bouts of filming at all hours of the day or night. Erich Kollmar tells of working for thirty-six hours straight at one point. Kollmar and Goldoni separately described to me one particular dark night of the soul near the end of the shoot. Cassavetes had arranged to film the 'dancing with Davey' scene late one night at Roseland. But when he and his small cast and crew showed up, they were told that they couldn't use the dance floor. After a little arguing and a lot of waiting, at one or two in the morning, they carried all of the equipment back to the Variety Arts building, and hurriedly rigged a few neutral flats and pointed a couple of spotlights at the stage to simulate a dance floor ambience, and filmed the scene there. Because of the change of location, they weren't finished until four in the morning. Unfortunately, arrangements had already been made to use Juliet's Corner for the Fountain scene at 6 a.m. Though Lelia Goldoni and several others protested vehemently, Cassavetes and Kollmar began filming two hours later. It is no wonder that Goldoni can be seen suppressing a yawn at the start.

Despite the around-the-clock nature of the reshoot (or perhaps because of it), the same party-like atmosphere prevailed as in the original shoot. Lelia Goldoni tells of being rattled (and more than a little shocked) by the goings-on in Cassavetes' livingroom prior to her big bedroom scene. She said she sat in the bedroom smoking and trying to compose herself for at least an hour while every member of the crew, led by the incorrigible Seymour Cassel, hung out of windows or climbed onto the roof of the building ogling and trying to get a better view of a shapely blonde in a state of undress in an apartment across the courtyard. Cassavetes then got on the phone and persuaded her to appear in the party scene to be filmed the next day. It turned out she was a former Miss Denmark and sometime actress named Greta Thyssen, who became the star of the hilarious 'exotic dancer' bit.

More than 40,000 ft. (eighteen hours) of new footage were shot over a two-week period. With Maurice McEndree's and Len Appelson's continued help in the editing during the spring and summer of 1959, Cassavetes threw away approximately half of the old scenes (leaving less than twenty-five minutes of the original version remaining) and intercut almost an hour of new scenes into the film.

A Succès d'Estime
Cassavetes had the new version blown up to 35mm and gave it to Amos Vogel for its world première in two screenings on 11 November 1959 in a

programme entitled 'The Cinema of Improvisation' in Vogel's Cinema 16 series on 24th Street. *Shadows* was preceded on the programme by Robert Frank and Alfred Leslie's recently completed *Pull My Daisy* (which had itself been partially inspired by the Paris Theater screening of *Shadows* the year before). Vogel believed in the film so much that he paid Cassavetes a $250 rental, four or five times more than his usual amount. Having spent approximately $40,000 of his own money and three years of his life on the film at this point, it was the first penny of return Cassavetes

January 19, 1960

Mr. Amos Vogel
175 Lexington Avenue
New York 16, New York

Dear Amos:

Not being a terribly organized fellow and not being terribly proud of it, but simply wishing to underline the importance of your interest in "Shadows", I would like to thank you for your continued support. I received several offers for festivals for the picture which were very generous to say the least. Your letters regarding the reception that the film received at Cinema 16, along with the many that were sent to me because of the screening, certainly helped to fill the expectations that we all had for the film when we originally started.

Due to a misunderstanding that has arisen between Dave Horne and myself regarding his status in the film, I feel that I am unable at this time to send the picture anywhere, and therefore, it is at present in limbo. However, I screened "Shadows" for Cecil Smith, who is international editor of the Los Angeles Times in California, and he was heartily in favor of the film and deeply moved by its intention. He will have a piece on "Shadows" appearing in the Times (Los Angeles, that is) on January 24th. I will get copies of the article and send them to you.

Albert Johnson of the Film Quarterly Magazine of the University of California, who is the American correspondent of the British Quarterly, Sight and Sound, is doing a review in the Quarterly out March 1st and also doing an article in Sight and Sound mainly concerned with "Shadows". On May 4th, I would like to show "Shadows" as part of a campus lecture program. I am to call him to give him more information and I will not forget to send you copies of his comments.

You mentioned that Louis Malle had seen "Shadows" and stated that he would be helpful in the French distribution of the picture. Could you enlighten me further as to that conversation, as Seymour Castle at times is quite uncommunicative. There have been numerous requests in California for a screening and I am in a quandary as to how to proceed. I know that you are interested in "Shadows" and I certainly would appreciate your advice as to how to best distribute the picture in a non-commercial way that would benefit the purposes of experimental film.

As to the festivals and their interest, since we have been invited by some 10, namely, Vancouver, West German, Melbourne, Toronto, San Francisco, and several lesser festivals, I would like your opinion as to the possibilities of gaining entry into a festival such as Venice or Cannes. I feel very much, and have always felt,

Mr. Amos Vogel   2

that the Venice Film Festival was far and above the most extra-
ordinary. I feel also that this film would have the greatest
empathy with the judges at Venice, since "Shadows" contains,
in my opinion, much of that neo realistic influence.

Please advise me as to your feelings on the subject and thank
you once more for your continued interest.

                              Sincerely,

                              John Cassavetes

                              John Cassavetes

High hopes: Cassavetes was in California working on *Staccato* and unable to attend Vogel's
Cinema 16 screenings in New York (Courtesy Gena Rowlands)

had seen on his investment. The screenings were triumphs. The audience
of artists, critics and intellectuals, which included Parker Tyler, Paddy
Chayefsky, Kenneth Tynan, Meyer Shapiro and Arthur Knight (Louis
Malle had seen the film at a private screening a few days earlier),
responded with sustained ovations.

Hip and Square
The contrast between the two films on Vogel's programme is
illuminating. While *Shadows* uses figures like Lelia and Ben to
interrogate the adequacy of Beat stances and claims of freedom, *Pull
My Daisy* smugly, self-satisfyingly wallows in them. Frank's film simply
buys into Beat postures, while Cassavetes' attempts to understand them
and explore their emotional causes and consequences. *Shadows* is the
rarest of works from that period – a film that analyses the fraudulence of
Beat posturing, even as it appreciates why figures would want to protect
themselves in this way. Imaginatively positioning itself half-inside, half-
outside the Beat milieu, it reveals what is wrong with attempting to be
hip and detached, while continuing to love the characters despite their
flaws.

As is the case in so many Beat works (the films of Ron Rice and Ken
Jacobs serving as relevant reference points), the actors in *Pull My Daisy*
are in love with their own cuteness. They are ironic postmodernists before
the fact – turning all of life into a jokesy 'goof' or 'lark'. Cassavetes, on
the other hand, is a deadly serious film-maker (which doesn't prevent him

from being hilarious as well). *Pull My Daisy* may be charming and fun, but it is ultimately a frivolous work, because it imagines creativity as off to the side of the 'real world', something that you do on your days off – spouting doggerel and clowning around at home. For Cassavetes, the world is the place where you express your imagination. Lelia's theatricality, like Mabel's or Myrtle's later, represents an enrichment of ordinary, everyday life, not an alternative to it or a vacation from it. *Shadows* may be funny but is never a joke. Lelia, Tony and Ben show us that our words and actions have serious consequences.

Film-making as Thinking

Although Cassavetes and Aurthur may have begun by simply attempting to make *Shadows* feel less episodic, the new scenes (and the respositionings of old ones) completely changed the film. A comparison of the two versions, to the extent we are able to induce what the earlier one looked like, provides a rare glimpse of Cassavetes' mind at work. He appears to have studied his characters and their situations and changed his understanding of them. The first point to notice is that the additions are not about racial issues but characters' feelings. The drama moves inward. Characters are given depths of self-awareness that were largely absent from the first version.

Each of the characters is made more sympathetic by being given at least two new scenes which complicate our feelings about them. Hugh is no longer merely a failed musician who squabbles with his brother and manager, but is seen in caring encounters with Ben (in the rehearsal studio scene), Lelia (in the bus station and bedroom scenes) and Rupert (in the final Grand Central scene). Hugh's professional problem is also changed. In the earlier version, it was largely a question of how much money he made and his struggle with Rupert for control of his career. The additions to the rehearsal hall and joke-rehearsal scenes shift the issue from a professional disagreement to feelings of humiliation (and change the entire meaning of the nightclub debacle). The final Grand Central scene between Rupert and Hugh similarly moves Rupert's drama inward, away from being a struggle with Hugh to raising questions of self-doubt.

The additions move Ben's personality beyond his earlier narcissism and morbidness. The 'mask' moment at the Museum of Modern Art allows him to be thoughtful and sensitive. The Fountain scene gives him a playful side and allows him to express a tiny bit of ironic self-awareness of his imitative relation to 'Beat generation jazz'. (The only moment in the entire first version in which Ben and his buddies interacted in this lightly joking and playful manner was the brief card-playing scene; everywhere else they were either spoiling for fights or trying to pick up girls.) In the bedroom conversation with Lelia and Hugh, although Ben is still a bit of a poser ('I think I'll join a little group in Vegas'), he displays a sense of humour and seems genuinely concerned about Lelia. Cassavetes' editorial decision not to place the 'Charge' scene where he had originally intended it to fall, where it would show that Ben took the money he borrowed from Hugh and squandered it on beer and girls, is a further attempt to meliorate his presentation. The movement of the rock-and-roll scene from its original place after the fight with Jackie and Hugh, to under the credits at the beginning of the film, is another effort to prevent the viewer from taking a more critical stance toward Ben's behaviour.

Lelia's part was enlarged most of all. The added scenes bring out whole new sides of her personality: her sexual curiosity (the movie-theatre scene); the diffidence her flirtatiousness camouflages (in the sidewalk scene); her naivety (in the post-coital scene); her deep pain and remorse (in both bedroom scenes). Cassavetes did more than enlarge Lelia's part; the revision shifts the film's point of view. The first version focused on the male side of life and issues in the male characters' lives: Hugh's professional problems with Rupert; Ben's Œdipal struggle with Hugh, interactions with his buddies and relation to girls. Lelia (and the girls Ben flirts with) existed chiefly to cause problems for one of the men – to pit Tony against David; to allow Tony to turn on his seducer's act; to create problems for Davey to deal with. In the second version, Lelia not only replaces Ben as the main character, but the male bias of the earlier story is eliminated. The woman's side of the story is given its due.

Even Tony is slightly revised upwards. It's indicative of his function in the first version that his character was referred to as 'the bigot', but it is impossible to describe him that way in the second version. In the taxi scene, the call from the payphone, and the added apology shots, he is genuinely concerned about Lelia's feelings. The payphone shot was present in the earlier version, but was used for the opposite purpose. Tony called David to tell him that Lelia had 'forced herself' on him and that it wasn't his fault they had sex. It was the portrait of a much more conventional seducer.

At the same time, it is critical that the new scenes didn't simply replace the old ones, but were intercut *between* them. The different views of the characters (immature and mature, careless and thoughtful, narcissistic and responsible, comic and serious) are *both* present, on top of each other as it were. Identity is cubistic. Individuals do not have one self, but many. Truth is not synoptic, but additive.[26]

A Democratic Narrative

One of the hallmarks of Cassavetes' work is the multiple-stranded narrative. While Hollywood is premised on an identification strategy in which the viewer processes information in terms of a single, dominant understanding of what things mean (generally figured by the star's viewpoint, though the understanding may be shared with or parcelled out among several main characters), none of Cassavetes' films is organised in this way. Life contains many different stories and alternative points of view. The narrative circulates the viewer through alternative perspectives and relations to experience – no one of which is necessarily more important, virtuous or correct than any other.[27]

It is crucial to the effect of the film that *Shadows* tells three stories at once, and grants Hugh, Lelia and Ben independent identities, sets of friends, and problems to deal with. In a narrative paradigm that will be repeated in all of Cassavetes' subsequent films, the initial scenes present the characters separately so that the viewer can get to know and care about each as an individual; the middle section brings the figures together in extended interactions with each other so that differences in temperament and behaviour can be registered,[28] and the closing scenes separate the characters one final time and provide separate conclusions to their individual stories. The narrative even-handedness prevents any one figure from 'starring' or relegating the others to merely 'supporting' status. Though Lelia has more on-screen time than either of her brothers, in no sense can Hugh or Ben be said to be merely supporting figures in 'her' movie. No matter how gripping or painful her personal drama is, she is not allowed to take over the film and make it hers. The effect is simultaneously invigorating and chastening. The switches from one figure's story to another's keep each 'in his place'. Even as one character demands our attention and sympathy, the others make equally important and conflicting claims on our feelings.

Multiple-mindedness

> The reactions to leading performers were not modulated. In other words, if somebody had a smaller part he didn't have to bend to the film's superstar role and didn't have to listen to the hero's sad story.

What Cassavetes does macroscopically, he does microscopically. The photography and editing circulate the viewer through multiple points of view in the same way that the multiple-stranded narrative does. Consider the brief scene with the cabby. It comes at a moment at which the viewer has been deeply absorbed in Lelia and Tony's emotional situation uninterruptedly for almost ten minutes. So what does Cassavetes do? He has them get into a cab where the driver – with his complaints about 'my busy time', his sarcastic remarks ('Ain't love grand?') and singing ('I love you truly') – demands that they and we shift our attention to him and his situation. He may be kooky, but what makes the scene work is that the cabby is *right*: this is not the time or place for Lelia and Tony to be discussing their relationship, and real love does give the lie to love songs. As bizarre and unexpected as the moment is, we are forced to acknowledge the validity of *his* point of view. It's a small example of Cassavetes' ability to create a world of free and independent consciousnesses, where the protagonist does not necessarily set the tone or mood of a scene. It is a world where the story can fork down another narrative path at any moment, where a minor character can take over a scene and move it in a completely new direction.[29] Single-mindedness gives way to multiple-mindedness.

Maintaining multiple perspectives: most of *Shadows'* drama is generated by small, fleeting emotional events like Hugh's embarrassment and frustration here

Where Hollywood is centripetal, focusing ever more tightly in on a central figure or situation, Cassavetes is centrifugal. Focus gives way to circulation. At every point that the viewer is inclined to narrow his or her attention, Cassavetes broadens it. The rehearsal studio scene presents another illustration of the effect. Although Hugh's point of view is clearly the most important one, the master-shot photography keeps Ben's, Rupert's and Ackerman's views imaginatively present, and the cutting from face to face in the close-ups keeps reminding the viewer of others' perspectives. The virtuosic pan that ends the scene can stand as a summary of the emotional polyphony. Hugh turns away from his discouraging conversation with Ackerman and Rupert, and the camera and soundtrack take in, in succession: Rupert's face still partially visible behind Hugh in the background; Rupert and Ackerman's voices still audible on the soundtrack; Hugh's discouraged expression; the face of a girl behind him looking at him; Sam the piano player's wink at a girl in the chorus line; and, finally, the chorus girl's hand reaching in and touching Sam on the shoulder. Even at this moment, Hugh is not allowed to be the star of a one-man show. His story is one among many. His career may be dying, but the piano player is apparently starting a hot romance.[30]

Real Problems

> I'm trying to make a film about people and their problems – what their *real* problems are, not something that is created by an accident of life but something we can control.

While most American films define experience externally (we are what we do or what happens to us), the experiences that matter in a Cassavetes film are internal (not what we *do* but what we *are*). Characterisation replaces eventfulness. There are external actions and events in Cassavetes' work, but they are only epiphenomena of internal states. Lelia's squabbles with Hugh and David, sexual debacle with Tony and rudeness toward Davey are windows into her soul. Ben gets into fights or is unhappy because of who he *is*. The problem is never 'out there', and it is never really caused by someone else. When Cassavetes called them 'real problems', he intended the adjective in two senses of the word: they are the kind of problems we encounter in 'real' life; and they 'really' matter because we do them to ourselves. The problems in Hollywood movies – rescuing the hostages, winning the race, getting the girl – are 'accidental' not only because they seldom occur in life, but because they are not involved with the essence of our natures.

Cassavetes gets himself into trouble with viewers on two counts, however. In the first place, external problems are much easier for audiences to perceive and follow. Characters' progress towards a solution (or failure to progress) can be measured in a virtually step-by-step way. Spiritual and emotional problems are far more elusive. What is Hugh's problem? Lelia's? Rupert's? Ben's? It may be a long while before a viewer can say. Second, when problems are imposed on characters from outside, situations can almost always be glossed in terms of a series of clear-cut moral oppositions. The characters who cause the problem become bad guys and the ones who solve it become good. Situations and actions are amenable to ethical judgement. When characters cause their own problems, moral evaluations become much less tenable. Everyone in a Cassavetes film is imperfect and flawed to some extent; there are no heroes or villains; black and white give way to grey in-betweenness. There is a justice structure to Cassavetes' work. If you mistake your true feelings and emotional needs, you will suffer. But an external agent doesn't judge or punish you; you inflict the punishment on yourself. You get what you are. Figures like Lelia and Tony don't prompt us to judge them, but to understand them. Moral judgements are replaced by acts of sympathy and caring.

Non-ideological Understanding

> I feel that people are ultimately individuals and it's only when they are trained to fit into a sociological pattern that is convenient to someone that they begin to blame their conditions [on things outside themselves]. All my pictures are ... about individuals. That's the only thing I believe in ... Groups can go fuck themselves. All of them. You know, a black to me is a black. And when he's a person, he's a person. And when a Puerto Rican is a 'Puerto Rican' or a 'Hispanic' – I don't care what title [they put] on – to me there's a name for each person. I think it's marvelous to have a name. And a woman is not a 'woman'. It's either Gena or my mother or some person.

Insofar as Cassavetes defines experience in terms of internal states, his films resist 'ideological' or 'sociological' analysis, which invariably defines characters' relations to the world in terms of external systems of power and dominance. To the ideological critic, experience becomes its *outsides*; while Cassavetes defines it in terms of its *insides* – characters' insecurities, needs for approval, fears, desires to be independent. In Cassavetes' imaginative universe, the deepest, most important aspects of his figures' identities completely elude external systems of scrutiny and control. That is why Cassavetes' narratives are so indifferent to social, economic or political concerns. If we ask how the siblings in *Shadows* support themselves or how they can afford the furniture in Lelia's bedroom, we are asking the wrong questions. The allusions to Ben's unemployment or Hugh's underemployment exist to create emotional issues they must deal with, not financial ones. The problems the characters undergo do not originate in economic, political or social systems, but from their unacknowledged needs and desires.[31]

Cassavetes' understanding of life was colour-blind, class-blind and individualistic. *Shadows'* racial theme might seem flatly to contradict this line of argumentation, but in fact Cassavetes completely rejected any interpretation of *Shadows* that viewed the film in terms of race relations, precisely because it located Ben's, Hugh's or Lelia's problems outside themselves. In his own words, the film was not about racial but *'human* problems'.[32] Of course, it's not necessary to take his word for it; *Shadows* is its own best guide to how it should be understood. And what the film makes abundantly clear is that although Ben and Lelia would undoubtedly blame their problems on racism or others, their only real problems are themselves. Their racial confusions pale in comparison with (and in fact are only as a kind of metaphor for) emotional confusions that have nothing to do with race.[33]

While ideological analysis subtly downplays the importance of individual differences, Cassavetes maximises them. His characters are nothing in general and everything in particular. They are too idiosyncratic and eccentric to be representatives of anything. Or to put it conversely: if we cut Ben, Lelia and Hugh (or, later, the salesmen in *Faces* or Robert Harmon in *Love Streams*) to fit within the Procrustean bed of an ideological understanding, we would be lopping off everything that makes them interesting.

The Performer as Meaning-maker
Shadows creates meanings in a fundamentally different way from most other art films. Movies like *Citizen Kane*, *Psycho*, *2001* and *Apocalypse Now* employ generalised stylistic effects (lighting, lens choice, camera movement and placement, the composition of the frame space, symbolic props and various other formal devices) to make meanings. Cassavetes,

in contrast, tends to put the camera at eye level and fill-light most of his scenes. His meanings do not emanate from visual or acoustic effects, but from the performers' faces, bodies and voices. The difference makes all the difference in the world – and is probably responsible for much of the confusion that, even at this late date in film history, still dogs the critical appreciation of his films – the feeling that, whatever their virtues, they are not quite as carefully crafted or as well thought-out as the other kind of film.

In comparison with the cleverness of a stylistic presentation of knowledge, a work that relies on performance to create meaning may appear to be simple or glib. Cassavetes' films are anything but. In fact, they ask viewers and characters to enter into a more arduous, more complex and less resolved relationship to experience than the other kind of work does, because they deny the viewer an Archimedean stylistic point outside of the perceptual flow by which he can get theoretical leverage on it. Cassavetes is doing nothing less than offering a new understanding of experience.

Conceptions and Perceptions
Stylistic forms of presentation are predicated upon acts of metaphoric translation – inveterate, pervasive movements from perception to conception. Stylistic effects make 'points' about characters and experiences. They tell viewers what to notice and how to interpret it. They allow viewers to ride just above an experience, a little outside of it, slightly disengaged from it. The result is a slight but decisive state of abstraction. The world is held at arm's length. Its tangibility and physicality is slightly attenuated. Cassavetes' work denies that cognitive and emotional distance. The viewer isn't outside experience, learning *about* it, but up to his eyeballs swimming *in* it (in later works like *Faces* and *A Woman Under the Influence*, drowning in it, overwhelmed with the intensity and mercuriality of the emotional transactions). As in the most demanding forms of jazz performance, there is a wilful denial of conceptual release from the perceptual flux.[34]

Putting Plato in his Place
It's not too much to argue that the two kinds of film-making imagine different ways of being in the world. The stylistically inflected film figures an 'idealist' conception of meaning in which the visible world of people, places and things becomes the repository of imaginative meanings. The point is to look past the surfaces of life to take in 'deep'

Continuous, subtle shifts of
feeling and relationship –
meanings that won't stand
still to have a metaphoric
or stylistic snap-shot taken

significances. Characters' *insides*, their thoughts and feelings, become more important than their *outsides*, what they say or do. Experience is transformed into a mental event.

In Cassavetes' work, meaning is not somewhere behind everyday social and verbal interactions, but is *in* them. Relationships are not mental, but practical. Ben, Hugh, Lelia, Rupert and Tony do not have abstract imaginative relationships with each other and *Shadows* does not ask the viewer to have an abstract, imaginative relationship with them. Meaning is expressed through practical social and verbal interaction. Characters' supreme achievements are not imaginative and intellectual acts of *understanding*, but sensitive, caring acts of *expression*.[35]

Meanings in Motion

Performed meanings, at least those with the particularity and mutability of the ones Cassavetes presents, are almost always more complex than stylistically created meanings. While stylistic meanings are generic, performed meanings are comprised of particulars which cannot be generalised. They won't yield abstract or summary formations. They will not stop moving long enough to be stylistically glossed. They shift and flow. *Shadows* plunges its viewers and characters into a world of exhilaratingly, scarily shifting meanings and relationships. In Lelia and Tony's three conversations, they cycle through more than twenty different tonal relationships with each other. The three-minute joke scene between Rupert, Hugh and Sam takes in at least eight or ten different emotional beats and relationships between the three figures. The Fountain scene and the bedroom scene redeploy the characters in dozens of shifting alliances and different emotional relationships. There are no rest stops on this journey. The viewer must surf the outer edge of a continuously shifting wave of perceptual experience. We may be able to understand *Shadows* backwards, but we live it forwards, piecing things together as we go along.

Mysterious Experiences

The experiences in *Shadows* are mysterious – not only to a viewer but to the characters.[36] We do not know exactly why Hugh decides to take the job he doesn't want to take, why Lelia chooses to sleep with Tony, or why Ben fights with Hugh – and Hugh, Lelia and Ben probably couldn't tell us either. While most other films are busy nailing things down, declaring meanings, telling viewers what to think and feel, Cassavetes' leaves his characters and scenes slightly underinterpreted.

They are allowed to retain the multivalence and vagueness of people and events outside of the movies. It's a wonderful place to get a dramatic work to – a place like life.

It would have been easy for Cassavetes to have offered a psychological key to the characters and their relationships early in the film – to have turned Ben into a 'drifter', Lelia into a 'flirt' and Hugh into a 'frustrated failure'. All it would have taken would be a summarising verbal statement by the characters themselves or the slightest exaggeration in the way each is presented. Cassavetes withholds clarifying causal explanations.

Characters have many different sides and relationships that don't necessarily add up. Think of how we get to know Lelia. When we first meet her, in the train station scene with Hugh, she seems caring and responsible ('I forgot to pack your toothbrush ...') and protective ('You're going to be late ...'). Her assertions that Hugh should not worry about her seem justified. She seems strong, intelligent and mature. The scene in front of the movie theatre displays a totally different side of her personality. In disobeying Hugh, she shows that she has a mind of her own, but also seems extremely naive. (Brigitte Bardot clearly defines the limits of her erotic imagination.) The Fountain scene gives us yet another side of her, as she rallies and verbally spars with her brother and David. When she theatrically kisses Tony at the party, we get still another side of her. But if we are about to conclude that she is an irresponsible flirt, we are forced to change our minds a moment later when she sassily declines Tony's request to leave with him. A few minutes later, the pavement scene reveals still another side of her. She seems genuinely vulnerable and innocent.

Ben's personality is similarly never allowed to stabilise. There are many Bens. In the credits sequence at the rock and roll party, he seems shy and cowed – we do not know why. In the horseplay on the pavement, he seems innocently fun-loving and boyish. In the scene with his buddies and the three girls, he may be 'playing it cool', but his clumsiness and vulnerability (and self-deprecating wit – 'I think I'm stuck in this booth') makes his posing seem endearing. The Fountain and Museum of Modern Art sculpture garden scenes show him not only to be intelligent and self-reflective but to have a sense of humour. We can't corral him within a reductive generalisation. In later scenes, we can't really jeer at him even when he seems to take himself too seriously, since we also take him at least a little bit seriously.

Identities and Relationships in Flux

Cassavetes' characters contain multitudes (though in an entirely less insouciant, more strenuous and more perilous way than Whitman imagined). They turn on a dime emotionally – changing their minds, their tones, their moods in a heartbeat – kind, thoughtful, tender, vulnerable, witty or playful at one moment, tough, cynical, critical, hurt or threatened an instant later. That's why so many of Cassavetes' leading figures – Lelia here, but later the salesmen in *Faces*, Mabel in *A Woman Under the Influence*, and Sarah in *Love Streams* – function like dramatic performers. Their fluxionality stands as a criticism of static or passive forms of selfhood.

Preventing Judgements

Cassavetes pitches scenes at tonal in-between points that prevent conclusive or limiting judgements – especially negative ones. The use of comedy was one of Cassavetes' favourite ways of doing this throughout his career. Though the few essays that have been written about *Shadows*[37] seem to be completely tone deaf to this aspect of the film, most of *Shadows* is semi-comic. The comedy prevents moralistic readings. A viewer is too entertained by Ben and his buddies' comical clumsiness in the scene in which they attempt to pick up the three girls to be too hard on any of them. The zaniness of Tony and Lelia's flight from David through Central Park deflects ethical understandings. The delicate, semi-comic awkwardness of Lelia and Tony's post-coital conversation forces us to care, where we might otherwise have simply judged. Even if the rest of the film didn't exist, the fight scene alone makes it perfectly clear that Cassavetes knew what he was doing tonally. As a mere event (played silently on the VCR), it is horrifically realistic. (One of the standard workshop exercises involved creating a 'non-Hollywood' fight scene.) But the comically syncopated musical soundtrack, nutty verbal outbursts and close-ups (e.g. the 'My eye! My eye!' moment), and humorously spastic gestures at the conclusion change everything. It plays like the Keystone Cops.

All of these moments illustrate Cassavetes' point when he once said he preferred comedy to serious drama, 'because there are more different feelings' in comedy. His point is *not* to not take these scenes seriously. It's to not take them *only* seriously. He wants us to be as multiple-minded tonally as his narrative is dramatically: to hold more than one feeling in our hearts at a time – seeing absurdity and silliness at the same time we see seriousness.

Active Viewing

The irresolution of characters' identities, the slipperiness of their relationships, and the tonal in-betweenness of their interactions communicate a stunningly open-ended vision of experience. Nothing is written in stone; everything flows and changes. It's impossible to predict the next beat in any interaction. Nothing is preordained. Seemingly anything can happen at any moment. Precisely because it doesn't pre-digest and simplify experience, Cassavetes' work makes almost unprecedented demands on the viewer, who is confronted with the same sort of emotional and cognitive challenges with which the characters are confronted. *Shadows* asks its characters to hold themselves subtly responsive to unresolved, open-ended experiences, and it asks its viewers to do the same thing. Cassavetes' films are not merely descriptive, but *functional*. Their ultimate goal is not only to shake up their characters, but their viewers. They force the viewer out of his or her state of passivity, to engage him or herself actively with unglossed, unassimilated experiences. The demands are frankly in excess of many viewers' capacities. They want to lock into a fixed view of a character, a set tone for a scene, a static understanding of a relationship; not to have to keep changing their minds and adjusting their views.

Trapped in Self-imposed Roles

One of Cassavetes' and Lane's avowed goals when they founded the workshop was to help their actors break free from conventional forms of dramatic expression. But the conventions that mattered most to Cassavetes were those in life. One of the abiding principles of all of his work is that people are as trapped in artificial feelings in life as actors are on stage. Each of the main characters in *Shadows* might be said to be 'playing' a limiting 'role' or 'part'. (Insofar as Cassavetes viewed acting as being absolutely continuous with living, the theatrical metaphor is completely appropriate.) Lelia's is her pretence of worldliness and sophistication in the early part of the film and her subsequent indication that she does not need anyone. Hugh's is his image of himself as a self-abnegating protector who can take care of everyone. Ben's is his 'cool-man-cool' pose. Tony's is his idea of himself as a lady-killing charmer.[38]

Synthetic Emotions

Cassavetes realised that when roles are played this consummately, they are deeper than consciousness. Ben's, Lelia's, Hugh's and Tony's problem

Hiding your feelings, pushing emotions into the subtext: Tony and Lelia putting on masks that   65
cover up embarrassment and awkwardness

is not the role-playing in itself, but that they do not know they are doing it. They have lost track of who they really are and what they really want. They deny their true feelings – not only to others but also to themselves. They are fooling themselves about what they really think and feel.

That was, after all, the interest of the improvisation that Cassavetes created as the seed from which *Shadows* grew on that first Sunday afternoon. Tony is possessed by racial panic, but denies it. Some of his denials are obviously lies made up to attempt to hide his feelings from Hugh, Rupert and Lelia: 'I have to go ... I have an appointment ...' But the more interesting denials are attempts to *tell himself* that he is doing nothing wrong: 'We'll have lunch tomorrow ... Remember, you *told* me to go ...' Almost all of Tony's subsequent behaviour in *Shadows* is pitched in this place of self-congratulatory self-delusion. He is playing a role that he doesn't know is a role. Look at the post-coital conversation in which he 'plays' the lover ('All right, baby'), the cab scene in which he 'plays' concerned (telling Lelia how much she means to him), or the final scene in which he appears and asks Ben to 'tell her I realize there's no difference between us ... Tell her she'll always mean a lot to me ...' Who is fooling whom in these scenes? Cassavetes understood that the lies we tell others are trivial, the ones that matter are the ones we tell ourselves. But, as Tony demonstrates, we are the last ones to be aware of those deceits.

Subtextual Realities
Shadows presents a continuous double text, in which characters' words and actions are almost always evasions of emotional realities. The motivational logic of scene after scene is not in what characters say they are doing but in an invisible emotional subtext that underpins their words and actions: Lelia's desire for independence pulls her away from David and into Tony's arms and motivates her later treatment of Davey. Ben's self-dramatising conception of himself as a 'little lost lamb' leads him into the world of street fights, one-night stands, drifting and squabbles with his brother. Hugh's need to be needed and desire to take care of his younger siblings (who do not really want or need his protection) leads him into various forms of self-inflicted humiliation.

These motivational undercurrents are so deeply buried that the characters are oblivious to them. In fact, it takes a long time even for a sensitive viewer to see them. The undemonstrativeness of the subtextualisation is everything. If Lelia's desire for independence were

The return of the repressed: pent-up emotions disrupt polite routines. Lelia yells at Ben. Ben lashes out at Jackie

narrowed to an emotional 'issue' (said about her by another character or by herself), she would become a cartoon character in a television drama. By the time Tony has his first conversation with her, it is appropriate for inner reasons that Lelia flirt with him to attempt to retaliate for David's criticisms of her. But her desire to assert herself is not reduced to the expression of a 'theme'; it stays almost subliminal. Her self-assertion will lead to the act that will ultimately undo her, but it is *almost* invisible to a viewer – as it is to Lelia herself. The undercurrents of feeling that motivate her behaviour are too deeply buried to surface as a verbal statement and too confused to become an 'intention'. They have the slightness and obliquity of life.

Masks and Faces

To borrow Burt Lane's metaphor from his critique of the Method, *Shadows* is a study of the problems characters' 'masks' get them into. All of the principal characters wear masks in attempts to hide their feelings from others and to protect themselves from pain. Their problems arise when they confuse the masks with their faces. Since the masks are lies they tell themselves about themselves, they are ultimately unsustainable. Their poses get them into trouble not only with others but, more importantly, with themselves. The problem is that while life flows, a mask is fixed; while life demands responsiveness to others, the mask only responds to the individual's own needs. Emotions change, but the mask is rigid. Cassavetes' work is thoroughly dramatic in the sense that he almost never has a character directly present his own personal viewpoint, but David is the exception that proves the rule in the Fountain scene, when he tells Ben that he is trapped in an emotional and behavioural 'pattern'. In Cassavetes' opinion, the real threats to our identities are always within ourselves. Our emotions always tend to congeal into a static, self-protective stance. We mechanise and regiment ourselves; it doesn't take racism, capitalism or bourgeois values to do it to us.[39]

Breakdowns and Breakthroughs

The drama within the drama of *Shadows* is the conflict between social surfaces and emotional depths. The mask slips off. The smile cracks. We cease to believe the story we tell ourselves to cheer ourselves up. The logic of *Shadows* is a logic of breakdown. Hugh puts on a brave face in the rehearsal hall and the nightclub scenes, but in the final shots of both scenes Cassavetes lets a viewer see the discouragement deep in his eyes.[40]

The discrepancy between the mask and the emotional reality is registered at other points in the film by paroxysms of anger or frustration. Hugh's 'big brother' composure can only be maintained for so long. He loses his temper first with Ben and subsequently with Rupert. Lelia explodes at Ben in the bedroom scene (when he innocently observes that she doesn't look very good after being up all night). Even the apparently unflappable Rupert has his moment of breakdown in the train station. Emotions that were kept bottled up suddenly bubble up to the surface.

Spiritual Insights

> There is a compromise made if you work on a commercial film and the compromise really isn't how or what you do, the techniques you use, or even the content, but really the compromise is beginning to feel a lack of confidence in your innermost thoughts. These innermost thoughts become less and less a part of you and once you lose them then you don't have anything else. I found myself losing them too, and then suddenly I woke up by accident, by sheer accident of not getting along with something, something inside.

The revised version of *Shadows* ends with three successive 'recognition' scenes (two of which were not in the 1958 print) in which Lelia (dancing with Davey), Hugh and Rupert (in Grand Central), and Ben (in a bar with his buddies) are forced to admit their emotional needs. In a typically Cassavetean narrative development, all four characters briefly stop being cool, calm, composed or aloof, and allow their feelings to show. This final narrative movement, like all of the important moments that precede it in *Shadows*, represents an essentially inward dramatic event. It's not about action but insight.

As in classic Greek drama, *Shadows* ends with moments of *anagnorisis*. Characters realise things about themselves – not by thinking but by listening to their hearts. Like Cassavetes himself in 1956, when he began the dramatic workshop with Lane, they wake up because they dare to stop playing a role they are uncomfortable with and finally listen to a voice of discontent that may have been nagging away for years. All of Cassavetes' work is about learning to hear that still, small voice. He was a deeply spiritual artist – like Bresson, Tarkovsky and Dreyer, a religious film-maker in a post-religious age. He was an artist of hope – a poet of the miraculous, transforming power of emotion to teach us things our minds are slow to learn.

Shadows ends with a series of epiphanies and recognitions: Lelia's mask of self-confidence slips off and her real feelings emerge

Postscript

Shadows is one of the minor masterworks of American art, but America is a difficult place for an artist to succeed at any time, and in the late 50s and early 60s, the concept of an 'art film' was unheard of outside of New York, Los Angeles and San Francisco. Following its London première, *Shadows* had financially successful runs in France, Denmark, Finland, Sweden and Italy. But, to Cassavetes' surprise and dismay, he found himself still unable to interest a single American distributor. The film was considered too 'experimental' in its narrative and too rough in its production values for American audiences. To add injury to insult, twenty members of the cast and crew launched a class-action lawsuit against him because the contract he had negotiated with British Lion cut their participation in the profits. Cassavetes, on his part, claimed it was years before he recouped the money he had put into the film and began to show the first dollar of profit.

After spending months unsuccessfully attempting to secure American distribution, Cassavetes reluctantly signed a deal for the London releaser, British Lion, to handle the film in the United States. It was the first time the company had ever attempted to distribute a film in America and, if truth be told, it was not very good at it. The company presented the movie to scores of exhibitors at screenings between January and July of 1961. Only three theatres, the Embassy in New York and the Sunset and Crest in Los Angeles, were willing to commit to commercial bookings. *Shadows* played for a few weeks at each to generally empty houses. After July, the prints were returned to Cassavetes and put into storage. There would be no more bookings or requests to screen the film for years. A decade later, Cassavetes summarised the situation that many a subsequent American independent film-maker has experienced:

> All that tremendous hoopla stayed on the other side of the Atlantic, I'm sorry to say. In America, we had what we started out with – a 16mm, black-and-white, grainy, rule-breaking, nonimportant film that got shown only when someone was willing to do us a favor.

APPENDIX:
A COMPARISON OF THE TWO VERSIONS OF 'SHADOWS'

· ·

Sequential time (from the first frame of the 1959 print)	Year scene was filmed	Summary of the shot, scene or sequence	Basis for the dating (see Key #1)	Other notes (see Key #2)
0–2:06	1957	A rock and roll party. The credits. Ben makes his way through the crowd and cowers in the corner.	BC, v	1, 2, 3, 39
Cut	1957	The initial scene of the 1958 print. Old friends Tony and David meet on the street, and David invites Tony to his party.	a	4
2:06–2:18	1957	'Most happy fella.' Ben walks down the street.	BC, b	5, 6
Cut	1957	David and Lelia go into a pharmacy and David caresses Lelia's hair.	c	
2:18–2:59	1959	'Charge' scene: Ben runs up to Tom and Dennis with twenty dollars; a fight ensues with a friend.	BC, DS, TA	7, 8, 9
3:00–6:16	1957	Ben, Tom and Dennis go into a bar and talk with three girls.	BC, DS, TA, d	42
6:16–6:56	1957	Ben walks down the street and into the entrance of a building.	BC	5
6:56–10:41	1959	Ben goes inside the rehearsal hall and asks Hugh for money while Hugh argues with Rupert and Ackerman.	JA, BC, HH, d, e, f, g	9, 10, 11, 12, 13, 14, 15
8:14–10:10	1957	Four shots from the 1957 shoot are edited into the rehearsal hall sequence at 8:14-8:20; 9:21–9:31; 9:35–9:49; 9:49–10:10.	JA, BC, HH, e, f, h	11, 39
10:41–11:56	1959	Lelia sees Hugh off at Grand Central.	HH, LG, d, i	16, 17
11:56–12:26	1957	Hugh runs through Grand Central, meets Rupert, and they run for a bus.	HH, i	6
12:26–13:48	1959	Lelia walks past movie theatres and is accosted by a stranger.	LG, d, j, k	6, 17, 18
13:48–16:56	1959	Hugh, Sam and Rupert rehearse jokes in Sam's apartment.	k, l	9, 10, 14, 19, 20, 21
Cut	1957	The nightclub dressing-room: the girls talk and prepare for the show; Hugh, Rupert and Ackerman argue in the background.		14
16:56–19:34	1957	The nightclub. Two comedians perform; Rupert and Ackerman watch Hugh on stage; the girlie line comes out.	JA, f, g, h, s	21, 22, 23, 24, 25, 39
19:34–23:10	1959	Fountain scene. David, Lelia, Ben, Tom and Dennis.	BC, DS, TA, LG, DP, d	17, 26
23:11–26:01	1959	Ben, Tom and Dennis in the Museum of Modern Art sculpture garden.	BC, DS, TA, d, m, n	27, 28
26:01–29:01	1959	David's literary party. Tony tries to pick up various girls.	LG, DP, TR, k, o, p	19
29:01–31:21	1959	David, Lelia and Tony converse at David's party.	LG, DP, TR, d, k	10, 17, 19, 29

Sequential time (from the first frame of the 1959 print)	Year scene was filmed	Summary of the shot, scene or sequence	Basis for the dating (see Key #1)	Other notes (see Key #2)
31:21–32:51	1957	David, Lelia and Tony walk through Central Park; Moe-Moe greets them; Lelia and Tony run away.	LG, DP, TR, d	
32:51–34:46	1959	Lelia and Tony on the street in front of his apartment.	LG, TR, d, k	
34:46–36:36	1959	Lelia and Tony in Tony's apartment hugging and kissing.	LG, TR, d, q	
36:36–40:16	1959	Post-coital. Lelia and Tony in bed.	LG, TR, d, k, n, r	17, 27, 29
40:16–41:41	1959	Lelia and Tony and the cabby.	LG, TR, d, k, r	17, 30
41:41–48:25	1957	At the Carruthers apartment: the three boys play cards and make a phone call; Lelia and Tony dance and lie on the couch together; Hugh and Rupert unexpectedly enter; discovering Lelia's race, Tony says he has to go.	BC, DS, TA, LG, TR, HH, d, s, t	22, 31, 32
48:25–48:32	1957	Tony makes a phone call.	u	33
48:32–49:14	1959	Lelia lies in bed listening to the phone ring and says good night to Hugh.	LG, d	19
49:15–49:27	1959	Ben hears Hugh's alarm and gets up.	BC	19
49:28–49:36	1959	Hugh turns off his alarm and gets up.		19
49:37–53:16	1959	Lelia lies in bed, while Ben and Hugh interact with her outside the bathroom.	LG, d, k	9, 15, 16, 19, 34
53:16–58:28	1957	Hugh's party; Lelia talks with Vickie and meets Davey; David apologises for Tony; Jackie talks with Ben; Ben and Hugh fight.	LG, BC, HH, d, p, s, t	15
58:28–58:56	1957	'Mary had a little lamb' scene. Ben goes down into the basement club.	BC, d, v	
58:56–1:00:46	1957	Hugh and Rupert talk with their girlfriends until the early hours of the morning.	HH, k, p, t	22
1:00:46–1:01:38	1957	Ben returns and he and Hugh make up.	BC, HH, t	15
1:01:38–1:08:24	1957	Davey arrives for his date; Lelia keeps him waiting; Tony shows up as she leaves and apologises; Ben and Hugh interact.	LG, BC TR, DJ, d, k, s, w	22, 35
1:06:56–1:07:36	1959	Five shots of Ben and five of Tony are interpolated during the apology sequence.	BC, TR, t, w	
1:08:25–1:10:46	1959	Davey and Lelia dance and share an intimate moment.	LG, DJ, d, k, r, t	10, 36, 37
1:10:47–1:11:04	1957	Hugh races through Grand Central Station.	HH, i	
1:11:05–1:13:29	1959	Hugh and Rupert share an intimate moment.	HH, g, i, x	36, 38
1:13:30–1:17:43	1957	'The Happiness Boys'. Ben, Tom and Dennis meet in a bar, try to pick up two girls, and get into a fight with three guys.	BC, DS TA, d	39, 40
1:17:43–1:18:40	1957	Ben, Tom and Dennis sit in a bar and Ben says he has learned a lesson.	BC, DS, TA, d	32
1:18:41–1:20:41	1957	Ben separates from the group and walks into the night. 'The film you have just seen was an improvisation.'	BC, d	2, 41

KEY #1:
HOW THE DATES OF SCENES WERE
DETERMINED

BC Ben used a sunlamp during the spring of
1957 and is tanned in all of the scenes from that
period (although the lighting occasionally
makes it hard to see). He had discontinued use of
it in 1959 and is much paler. The second
difference in Ben's appearance in the two shoots
is that during the 1957 shoot, he frequently wore
a light-coloured, V-neck sweater with three dark
stripes around the neckline, and less frequently a
beige crew-neck sweater. In the 1959 shoot, in
place of either of these sweaters, he wore a dark
navy sweater with a ribbed turtle-neck and a
variegated pattern just below the neckline,
across the upper chest area. The presence or
absence of any one of these three sweaters is an
absolute marker of the 1957 or 1959 shoot. The
light-coloured sweaters are visible in several
early scenes when his jacket is open at the top or
he is wearing a sport coat, and in scenes late in
the film when the sleeves or bottom hem of the
sweater extend beyond the sleeves or bottom
edge of his leather jacket. The dark-coloured
sweater is clearly visible in the rehearsal hall
scene. The only two sources of potential
confusion are that in the 1957 rehearsal hall
shots, Ben wears a dark-coloured turtle-neck
under his sport coat, and in several exterior
scenes in the 1957 shoot, Ben wears a dark scarf
under his jacket over the lighter-coloured,
triple-stripe V-neck sweater. Lelia Goldoni gave
it to him as a present during the first shoot and
any scene in which he wears the scarf around his
neck or carries it in his pocket positively dates
the scene as an early one. (He takes the scarf off
near the end of the movie and has it in his pocket
in some of the shots.) The third marker of the
two shoots is Ben's hair. In the 1957 shoot, he
wore his hair at two different lengths: long and
straight in a couple of the 1957 rehearsal hall
shots, but shorter, curlier, and more stringy in
his other 1957 scenes, including all of the ones
filmed on the Variety Arts stage, the early scene
with the three girls, and all of the scenes in the
final ten minutes of the film. (The reason for the
change of length is that early in the 1957 shoot,
but after the filming of the early version of the
rehearsal hall sequence, Cassavetes asked all
three boys to get haircuts.) In every scene of the
1959 shoot, Ben's hair is fairly long. The scenes
in the rehearsal hall, the Fountain and the
bedroom interaction with Lelia may be used as
reference points for the length of his hair at that
time. There are a few final, minor differences in
Ben's appearance in the two shoots. In the 1959
shoot, the left collar on his leather jacket has
curled over nearly in a complete circle, while in
the 1957 shoot, the curl has not progressed as far.
Ben wears white leather gloves in several of the

The 1957 literary party had a scene shot in the kitchen of Cassavetes' apartment; it is not in
the 1959 edit (© Sam Shaw)

scenes in the 1957 shoot but never during the reshoot. Finally, during some of the 1959 reshoot period he had a toothache and a slightly swollen cheek, and he occasionally turns his head away from the camera to mask the swelling or uses an ice pack to ease the pain (as in the Fountain scene).

DS Dennis Sallas' 1957 and 1959 scenes may be told apart by the condition of his trench coat, particularly the belt. In the first shoot, the coat appears to be new and the belt is smooth, lies flat around his waist, and is neatly buckled in the front. In the second shoot, the belt is twisted and folded, and secured by being knotted and tucked in on itself. Its 1957 appearance can be seen in the sequence in which Dennis walks into the restaurant where the boys meet the three girls near the start of the film and the sequence in the Carruthers apartment where the boys call the airline stewardess (both of which show the new coat with its flat, neatly laced belt). The scene in the MoMA sculpture garden shows what the coat and belt look like two years later. Dennis's face and hair change slightly in the two years between the shoots, but noticing the change requires becoming very familiar with his appearance through repeated viewings.

TA Tom wears the same dark crew-neck sweater over a white shirt with the collar out in each of the three scenes in which he appears in the reshoot (although he has a coat over his shirt and sweater in the 'Charge' scene). During the 1957 shoot his most frequent outfit is a white T-shirt, solid-colour sport shirt, and sport coat with a striped pattern to the fabric. The two sets of clothing are absolute markers of the two shoots. His hair is also slightly different in the two shoots. In 1957 it is slightly longer on top, unparted, and trimmed with clippers on the sides (freshly cut in the early scene with the three girls, the scene leading up to the fight and the fight scene, after Cassavetes had given the three boys money to get haircuts). In 1959, his hair is slightly shorter on top and his pompadour does not extend out as far in front, slightly longer on the sides (not trimmed with a clipper but combed back), and has a combed part on the right side. Tom's complexion is also ruddier and rougher in many scenes in the first shoot than the second.

HH Hugh's white cap is different in the two shoots. In the 1957 shoot, the hat has a plain back and the brim and front are secured with a single snap fastener; in the 1959 shoot, the hat has a small ornamental buckle at the back and the front of the hat is sewed onto the brim in a line. In the 1957 shoot, Hugh also looks slightly younger than he does in 1959. Hurd's hair is one of the hardest aspects of his appearance to read. It varied greatly during the 1957 shoot, ranging from long, shaggy, and unkempt in many of the on-stage scenes to quite short and neatly trimmed in the 1957 shots of the rehearsal studio scene.

JA Jack Ackerman, the impresario, wears a collar pin and light-coloured tie in the rehearsal studio and nightclub scenes in the 1957 shoot, but a straight collar and a darker tie in the 1959 reshoot.

LG By her own report, Lelia Goldoni's hair was approximately twice as long in 1957 as it was in 1959, mid-back length in the first shoot versus a little less than shoulder length in 1959. In the earlier shoot, she often wears her hair up in a braided bun; whereas in the 1959 shoot, she wears it gathered at the back or down (sometimes with a ribbon in it as in the bedroom scene in her apartment). Another major change in her appearance between the two versions is in the size and shape of her eyebrows. In the early shoot, they are thick and natural in shape; in the scripted version, they are much thinner and more finely sculpted. Goldoni also looks markedly thinner in 1959 than she does in 1957, having lost most of her baby fat in the two years between the shoots.

TR During the 1957 shoot Tony's hair was longer and thicker on top and less receded along the temples and sides than in the 1959 shoot. His face also looks younger and his body thinner in 1957 than 1959.

DP In the 1957 shoot, David Pokotilow's hair is short and neatly trimmed; in 1959, it is a little longer, and it sticks up higher and looks fairly wispy.

DJ Davey Jones wore a plain collar in the 1957 shoot, but a collar pin in the 1959 reshoot.

a David Pokotilow reported that this was the initial scene in the first version. His personal theory was that many of his scenes were cut because of his refusal to sign the new release contract; however it seems more likely that Cassavetes cut this and other scenes between David and Tony in order to downplay the 'male rivalry' side of the film and change Lelia's dramatic function.

b The Dean Martin film, *Ten Thousand Bedrooms*, is visible on a marquee. It opened in New York on 4 April 1957 and dates this sequence as almost certainly being shot that month (since filming wrapped in the middle of May). Cecil B. De Mille's *The Ten Commandments*, visible further back, began a long run in New York the previous November.

c Based on memory, Erich Kollmar and David Pokotilow verified that this scene was in the first version.

d Based on her memory, Lelia Goldoni has verified the date these scenes were shot.

e The rehearsal hall scene was present in both versions of the film, but the 1959 edit consists of almost entirely new shots, with only four shots retained from the earlier shoot (at: 8:14, 9:21, 9:35, and 9:49). The presence of Ben's dark sweater with the variegated pattern across the chest and the changes in Ackerman's collar and tie are the easiest ways to tell which shots are from which period of shooting. (See the entries for BC and JA.) Additional markers of the 1959 shoot: there are cups of coffee and one or two bottles of Pepsi on the piano; the hanger-on wearing sunglasses and a crew-neck sweater who cuts through the chorus line in an early shot is in the background of almost all of the subsequent shots; a girl wearing glasses is standing behind the piano; and a couple of the chorus girls from the 1959 group (one with a pony tail and one wearing a hat) are in the background of a few shots. Additional markers of the 1957 shoot: Hugh's hair is more neatly trimmed and slightly shorter than in the 1959 shots; there is a large striped scarf draped on the wall; and several of the girls from the 1957 chorus line are visible in the background or foreground of a few shots. (See item 'f' for more about the chorus line.)

f Maurice McEndree said that an attempt was made to obtain the same girls for the rehearsal hall chorus line in 1959 as were used in the nightclub chorus line in 1957, but locating them proved to be impossible. Gena Rowlands is a member of the 1957 rehearsal hall chorus line (but is not in the nightclub chorus line), and appears twice in the scene: once in the extreme left foreground when Ackerman says 'Shake your bodies around' at 8:17, and again, more fleetingly in the background of one of the shots with the scarf on the wall at 9:22. The only

reason Cassavetes included these two shots in the 1959 edit was to have Rowlands in the scene. (Rowlands couldn't appear in the 1959 shoot because she was six-months pregnant with the Cassavetes' first child.) Note that three of the chorus girls in the 1957 shoot are playing with ribbons that will be used in the nightclub scene, but that none of the ones in the 1959 shoot have similar props. (I would note that Maurice McEndree insists that everything in the rehearsal hall sequence was filmed in 1959, but it doesn't seem possible based on the above details.)

g Cassavetes rented a tricycle dolly for a few days during the 1959 shoot, and dolly shots help to establish the date.

h Because of problems obtaining permission to use Irving Berlin's music, Cassavetes looped 'A Real Mad Chick is Like a Lollipop' onto the soundtrack of the 1957 scenes and the figures in the earlier shoot are actually mouthing 'A Pretty Girl is Like a Melody' in both the rehearsal studio (at 8:17 when Ackerman sings the song) and the nightclub scene (when the girls sing it).

i Hugh's suitcase does not match the one in the 1959 shoot. It is lighter-coloured in the 1957 shoot, but darker in the reshoot.

j Lelia Goldoni is dressed identically to the previous scene. The films playing at the various theatres corroborate the spring 1959 shooting date. *The Night Heaven Fell* opened in New York on 22 October 1958, and the co-feature, *Man or Gun*, was a 1958 B-picture release starring MacDonald Carey. *Girls, Inc.*, directed by Barry Mahon, which is visible on a marquee at the end of the scene, is a 1959 film. The other films are re-runs of older pictures: Errol Flynn's *Desperate Journey* (1942), *Edge of Darkness* (1943), *Impulse* (1955), *Naked Paradise* (a 1957 feature) and *Naked Africa* (a 1957 documentary).

k The scripted dialogue is generally more witty in its effects and the interactions of the characters are more intricate than in the improvised version.

l The buttons in the men's tuxedo shirts are different from those in the nightclub scene.

m The three boys are dressed identically to the way they are in the 'Charge' scene and the scene in the fountain, and differently from the way they are dressed in any of the scenes in the 1957 shoot. Note Tom's hair and Dennis's trench coat in particular.

n In an article in *Film Culture* written at the time the second version was screened, Jonas Mekas notes that neither the post-coital scene nor the MoMA scene was in the 1957 film. Seymour Cassel, looking back fifty years later, insists that the MoMA scene was, but Mekas's contemporary account (and corroborations of it by Lelia Goldoni and Maurice McEndree) carry more weight. The presence of an unmarried couple in bed together and Tony's use of the word 'virgin' were objected to by a potential distributor when the first version was screened. In the 1959 shoot, Cassavetes had Tony say 'the first time' instead.

o Erich Kollmar and Lelia Goldoni verified that the literary party was present in both versions of the film, but was different. None of the shots from the 1957 filming was used in the 1959 print. Kollmar said that there were scenes in the kitchen and the bedroom (in the latter of which an Asian girl wandered into the room talking in a foreign language that no one understood). The kitchen is visible in production stills.

p Various minor characters visible in the group scenes, looking identical to the way they do in other shots, matched with major characters appearing as they do in the 1959 shoot, establish that the entire scene was filmed in 1959.

q A version of this scene was shot in 1957, but none of the shots was used in the 1959 edit. Lelia Goldoni describes the earlier version as a 'near rape' in which Tony seduced Lelia, repeatedly kissing and forcing himself on her sexually.

r Based on his memory of the reshoot, Seymour Cassel verified the date of this scene.

s The quality of the footage from the first shoot was often substandard. The negative shows scratches and other signs of poor handling.

t All of the scenes that take place in the living and dining rooms of the Carruthers apartment were filmed on the Variety Arts stage and are from the first shoot. The bookshelves, the dining room table with the light over it, the sofa, the Libby Holman poster, and the side entrance with the stanchion in the way are all markers of the 1957 shoot. The set was struck in May 1957. The stage was used in the reshoot only for the brief shots of Tony's apology and the dancing with Davey scenes which didn't involve the use of sets.

u Tony Ray told me that he remembered the phone call being added in 1959. But his memory is contradicted by the length of his hair, youthfulness of his face, and *Top Secret Affair* on the marquee in the background. The film opened in New York on 31 January 1957.

v In an article in *Film Culture* at the time the second version was released, Jonas Mekas says that the rock and roll party scene did not begin the first version. Since this scene was definitely filmed for the first version (based on Ben's hair, sweater, and drums), it probably continued the narrative after Ben goes down into the basement club.

w Tony's apology was shorter and more perfunctory in the 1957 version. Ben's shirt does not match the 1957 footage and Tony and Ben both look older in the 1959 shoot.

x It is likely that Cassavetes picked the spot because of the symbolic significance of the movie poster in the background advertising 'A Night to Remember'. It dates the scene since the film opened at the Criterion in New York on 17 December 1958. The buckle on Hugh's hat and the use of the dolly corroborate the date.

KEY #2:

MISCELLANEOUS POINTS ABOUT SCENES

1 In the 1958 edit, this scene did not appear in the credits sequence but probably followed the 'Mary had a little lamb scene' (at 58:28) where Ben goes down into the basement club. The move made Ben's character seem less narcissistic. In the scene's original position following Ben's fight with Jackie and Hugh, his cowering played as being petulant and self-absorbed. By being moved into the credits sequence, his actions are less narrowly defined. A viewer may be puzzled as to why he behaves this way, but does not judge him adversely. Cassavetes is briefly visible from behind nuzzling a girl during the appearance of the musical credit for 'Beautiful'. Seymour Cassel is briefly visible in several shots, drinking beer and looking directly into the camera. This scene is an illustration of the 'impressionistic' quality of many of the scenes in the 1958 print. Its montage effects would be much more striking if the scene did not run underneath the credits but occurred in its original position in the middle of the film.

2 Ben was not a trumpeter but a drummer in the first version. That is the reason he is carrying bongos in the first scene and has drum sticks in his back pocket in the last. Lelia Goldoni reported that he chose the instrument since he had fantasies of being a drummer, although he never learned to play. (In this respect he resembled his character.) It is probable that Cassavetes changed his instrument in the second version in order to be able to have him finger a trumpet in the bedroom scene. There is an inconsistency, however. In the bar scene with the three girls and three boys (which dates from 1957), he tells Nancy he plays the trumpet. Although the line may have been looped in 1959, it doesn't appear to have been.

3 Pir Marini is the pianist in both the rehearsal hall and nightclub scenes and the rock and roll scene.

4 Cassavetes was extremely jealous and rivalrous in romantic affairs and with other men in general. Much of the first version of the film focuses on situations involving male competition or rivalry: Ben's struggle with Hugh; Tony's with David; Ben's with Tony; Hugh's with Rupert. The reshoot moves away from this issue.

5 Note the mismatch in Ben's clothing in shots within these sequences from the 1957 shoot. Note also that some of the shots were taken from indoors through a plate glass window using a telephoto lens looking out on the street, so that the passers-by in the extreme foreground do not notice the camera.

6 One of the hazards of placing the camera in an environment with non-actors is that bystanders look into the lens.

7 Seymour Cassel is the figure in the light-coloured jacket who comes up to the boys and is punched at the end of the scene.

8 This scene was originally intended to follow the one in which Ben borrows money from Hugh, in which case its effect would have been completely different. It would have shown Ben's frivolousness with Hugh's hard-earned cash. In its current position, since viewers do not know how Ben obtained the money, they read it less moralistically. It plays not as financial irresponsibility but boyish horsing around. It is an illustration of Cassavetes' desire to avoid being too hard on Ben.

9 Note the close-figured two-, three- and four-shots in the rehearsal hall, the 'Charge' and the

joke-telling scenes, indicating that Cassavetes' desire to fill the frame and create visual interest continued unabated in the 1959 reshoot.

10 Many of Cassavetes' films employ variations on the idea that if you 'are yourself' you can't do wrong. It is introduced in several scenes.

11 The issue in the 1957 version of the rehearsal studio scene was strictly financial. Hugh argued with Ackerman and Rupert about the amount of money he was being offered. The 1959 shoot introduced the 'humiliation' issue. Hugh mentions the girlie line four times and Ackerman twice in the reshot or re-edited rehearsal hall footage at: 7:23; 7:34; 8:27; 9:04; 9:28 (looped into earlier footage); and 10:13.

12 Ackerman's improvised 'You're not infallible, you know' is probably indebted to the similar line in Reginald Rose's *Twelve Angry Men*. Ackerman is the weakest major actor in the film. His shoulder shrugs and twitches are self-conscious and clichéd.

13 Cassavetes puts his own sentiments in Rupert's mouth with the lines about being an artist at 8:31.

14 In the 1957 shoot Cassavetes included a back-stage scene in the nightclub dressing room in which, according to Maurice McEndree, the girls sat in the foreground putting on makeup, working crossword puzzles and talking, while Rupert, Hugh and Ackerman stood in the background arguing about Hugh's act. (Hugh's state of anger and frustration at this conversation is still apparent in the 1959 print for an instant as he comes on stage.) When Cassavetes added footage in 1959, he wanted to refilm this scene, but when the nightclub was not available, he created a new version of the rehearsal hall scene in its place and cut out the dressing-room scene. It's worth noting that *Too Late Blues*, *The Killing of a Chinese Bookie* and *Opening Night* have similar dressing-room scenes.

15 Ben's relationship with Hugh mirrors Cassavetes' own with his brother, Nick. In the early years of the decade, Cassavetes shamelessly mooched off his successful older brother, then watched in the final years of the decade as his brother underwent financial reverses and his career stalled. Nick died in 1958.

16 Lelia is made more responsible in the 1959 shoot. She looks out for her brother – packing Hugh's bags, seeing him off at the station, making sure he is not late and doesn't forget his suitcase, and doing laundry.

17 In the 1959 shoot, Lelia is less a victim and more a free and independent agent. Many of the added scenes are designed to display her independence.

18 Cassavetes is the man who protects Lelia. Nicos Papadakis, who raised some of the money for the reshoot, plays the masher. Lelia Goldoni pointed out that she slipped and fell after Papadakis came up to her and Papadakis briefly came out of character to help her up. As was often the case with Cassavetes' scenes, Goldoni didn't know how the scene would play out, and she reported that when Cassavetes stepped into the scene she didn't know if it was because she had fallen or if it was part of the scene.

19 Cassavetes used the livingroom, studio and two bedrooms of his penthouse apartment at 40 East 75th Street between Fifth and Madison for scenes in the reshoot. Various items identify the location. The furniture in the livingroom scene reappears in *Faces* and *Love Streams*. The stuffed tiger in the group scene belonged to Gena Rowlands. The Rouault painting belonged to Cassavetes. And the rooftop of the apartment is visible in the background of Ben's bedroom scene. As a side note, Bruce Dern was an actor who interested Cassavetes and was included in the background of the 1957 shoot of this scene; however, he was not present for the reshoot.

20 The reference to Steve Allen doesn't independently establish the date. *The Steve Allen Show* was broadcast on NBC from June 1956 through December 1961.

21 The joke-telling scene develops the 'humiliation' issue which the reshoot of the rehearsal hall scene had added to the film, changing how a viewer understands Hugh's nightclub appearance. In the 1957 shoot the question at stake was the success or failure of Hugh's act and his relation with Rupert. The 1959 reshoot moves the problem inward, to Hugh's feelings about himself.

22 Lelia Goldoni has verified that the nature of Hugh's artistic problem changes between the two versions. In the 1957 shoot, the issue was that Rupert wanted him to change his singing style and altered his arrangements. In the 1959 shoot, the issue is that his career is not succeeding. The final edit retains four allusions to the earlier issue from the 1957 film (e.g. Rupert's remark about '"Jelly Roll" sung like

an opera', and Hugh's resentment at how Rupert 'changed all the arrangements on me').

23 Sheldon Hackney and Danny Simon, Neil Simon's brother, play the comedians.

24 This scene was shot by Robert Rossen.

25 Jean Shepherd is sitting at a table in the nightclub scene. As the two comedians work the room at the start of the sequence and the camera pans with them, he is the man with a cigarette in his mouth at 17:04. His secretary, Ellen Paulos, who worked as a production assistant on the film, is the blonde sitting on the left side of the table with Gena Rowlands (and is the girl smiling at a male companion in a later shot).

26 David's comments about the importance of 'breaking patterns' echo Cassavetes' sentiments.

27 The 'mask' issue is made explicit in the 1959 shoot.

28 Note the condensation from the boys' breath, putting the date of filming in late February or early March.

29 Lelia's hairdo changes during the scene, indicating that more than one day was devoted to filming it.

30 The cab scene was filmed in a warehouse. Al Ruban remembers it being the last scene filmed in the reshoot. Erich Kollmar remembers the calculations involved with setting up the camera and lights and having the cab (driven by Bob Reeh who also built many of the sets on the Variety Arts stage) pull up to the camera by driving forward and then stopping as if it were letting Tony and Lelia out.

31 This scene was the origin of the film.

32 The fight scene and Ben's post-fight statement were moved to the end of the film in the re-edit. In the 1958 edit they occurred before the card game in the Carruthers apartment, which is why the signs of the fight are visible on the boys' faces in that scene.

33 In the original edit, Tony was not calling Lelia, but David to say that Lelia had seduced him and that it wasn't his fault that they had had sex.

34 This scene effectively uses the bathroom entrances and exits of the characters to change the conversational groupings.

35 This scene provides another illustration of the film's subtextual logic. Although nothing is directly said by Ben or Hugh about Tony, it is clear that the two brothers bond over their shared differences with him. They share a laugh at his comical behaviour.

36 Two scenes added in 1959 in which characters undergo self-recognitions.

37 Cassavetes wanted to film this scene on the dance floor at Roseland Dance City, but was forced to move it to the Variety Arts stage, where he simulated a ballroom by using a spotlight and a few flats.

38 Cassavetes is expressing his own personal sentiments when he has Hugh console Rupert and tell him that friendship is more important than business.

39 In the 1957 shoot, some of the actors who played minor roles played more than one part. Many of the dancers in the rock and roll club appear in the literary party. Several of the female guests at the literary party are in the nightclub chorus line. And the two actresses in the 'Happiness boys' scene late in the film, Carol Stern (a brunette) and Carrie Radison (a strawberry blonde), are also in the nightclub

chorus line (the first and fifth girls in the line). Also see note 3.

40 In the first edit, one of the boys had said 'Fuck you' during the fight scene. Cassavetes removed the words from the later edit as well as removing several shots in which 'Fuck you' was prominently visible in the background as a graffito on the wall of the dumpster (though it still is partially visible in several shots of the 1959 edit).

41 Shot with a telephoto lens from the roof of the Roseland building. George O'Halloran, who was an uncredited production and editorial assistant, says the camera shot through the 'O' in Roseland.

42 Filmed in Patsy Perroni's Bar. Erich Kollmar steps onto the other side of the camera to play the bartender at 3:10. Cliff Carnell and Carrie Radison play two of the customers. See note 39.

Characters who never directly say what they feel. A film of relentless emotional denials, suppressions, and expressive obliquities

NOTES

· ·

1 All quotations from John Cassavetes are taken from: Ray Carney (ed.), *Cassavetes on Cassavetes* (London: Faber & Faber, 2001).
2 This is incidentally why Rowlands had almost no involvement with and little knowledge of the activities at the workshop or the filming of *Shadows*.
3 There is an unconfirmed rumour that Cassavetes auditioned twice and was rejected twice prior to the event that I describe, and that one of the reasons he founded the workshop with Lane was because he was unable to get into Strasberg's group.
4 Burt Lane, 'Lane Workshop Now Runs Its Own Thr. Director Gives Critique of the Method', *Show Business*, June 1958, pp. 13–14.
5 Cassavetes was indebted to Lane for many dramatic ideas. Another was the belief that at the end of a work a character should undergo an 'epiphany' or 'recognition' of some sort. It was one of Lane's central dramatic beliefs which he and Cassavetes frequently discussed, and it later became one of the defining characteristics of Cassavetes' own films.
6 The workshop prided itself on being extremely 'progressive'. It was completely integrated and its members were fairly enlightened when it came to racial issues. However, subtle racial frictions still existed. Hugh Hurd told me of occasional remarks being made to him about the fact that he spent so much time with Lelia Goldoni, and of racial incidents outside the workshop that both he and Rupert Crosse experienced. The response to Martin Ritt's *Edge of the City* (which Cassavetes had acted in only six months earlier and which probably gave him the idea for the scene) is indicative of how touchy the racial issue was at the time. The film was picketed or banned in parts of the South simply because it depicted a friendship between a black and a white.
7 All of Cassavetes' films have similar scenes which put the actors in emotional situations which generally involve a discrepancy between the way the character is 'supposed' to behave (according to the rules of polite society), and what the character actually 'truthfully' feels, says or does. Consider *Faces*

as an example: Freddie's interaction with Jeannie, and Louise's with Chettie are similar in this respect to Tony's interaction with Lelia. Cassavetes was clearly interested in moments in which characters experience fears and insecurities which violate the rules of polite social expression and consequently lead to unformulaic and unpredictable interactions. *Husbands* and *A Woman Under the Influence* are organised around many similar moments.
8 Experiences of humiliation and embarrassment are central to Cassavetes' work. Hugh is embarrassed in his appearance at the nightclub. 'Ghost' Wakefield is embarrassed in front of a girl he is in love with in *Too Late Blues*. Maria, Freddie and Louise experience real or imagined embarrassments in various scenes in *Faces*. Archie feels that he has been sexually humiliated in *Husbands*, and Minnie is embarrassed by Zelmo and Seymour in *Minnie and Moskowitz*. Nick is embarrassed in front of his construction worker friends in *A Woman Under the Influence*. Cosmo and his double, Mr Sophistication, are afraid of being embarrassed in *The Killing of a Chinese Bookie*, and all of the main characters in *Opening Night* are motivated by fears of public humiliation.
9 The character of Cosmo Vitelli in *The Killing of a Chinese Bookie* is a related exploration of a man who does so much for others that he forgets about his own needs. It is likely that both Hugh and Cosmo are veiled portraits of Cassavetes' highly responsible and dutiful brother, Nick.
10 The film was entitled *Forgotten Glory* and was introduced by Sydney Poitier, with a script by David Pokotilow, but Kollmar says that he doubts that any prints survive.
11 The date of the broadcast is probably historically irrecoverable, but the best reconstruction is that since *Edge of the City* was released on 31 January and the ostensible reason for Cassavetes' appearance was to thank Shepherd for mentioning the film on his show a week or two earlier, the fund-raising pitch most likely occurred on either Sunday, 10 February or Sunday, 17 February. (Several sources confirm that it was on a Sunday night.)

12 Burt Lane was upset that he had not even been consulted or told in advance about any of this. He showed up on Monday and found the workshop – and its stage – taken over for a project of which he had no knowledge.

13 Cassavetes' descriptions in interviews of using a 'tape recorder' have given rise to the myth that the film's sound was recorded on non-synch equipment. However, the term is just a reference to the fact that the equipment used was not the older wire-recording system.

14 Erich Kollmar insists that no booms were used; however, there appears to be the shadow of a boom in at least two scenes: the one in which Ben returns Hugh's keys, and the scene in which Lelia keeps Davey Jones waiting.

15 The most extreme illustrations of overexposure are the scenes in which Tony and Lelia dance in her apartment and the scene in which Lelia keeps Davey Jones waiting. Both are from the initial period of shooting.

16 This is the statement I allude to in the introduction, in my mention of Cassavetes' frequent exaggerations and embellishments. No gun shots took place.

17 As an indication that Rupert's speech was scripted, some of his phrases crop up in Cassavetes' script of *Husbands* (as does Davey Jones' 'shake it up' comment when he wants Lelia to hurry up).

18 Cassavetes told an interviewer that he reversed the normal shooting pattern, where the master shot is done first and close-ups are done afterwards. He said that after he and his actors would discuss the scene and the relationships between the characters, close-ups on the individual actors would be shot first, while the actor worked out what he wanted to say and do (with other actors feeding him lines off-camera). After the dialogue and overall direction of the scene had been established, the master shot could be done more easily. Erich Kollmar denies that they proceeded in this way.

19 After Tony left the Carruthers apartment, Hugh had a moment in which he began to weep over the sadness and unfairness of racial divisions. Hugh Hurd remembered that one of his lines went something like: 'When I see my black hands against the white newspaper, I suddenly realize what I am.' He told me when he started crying as the moment was being filmed, everyone else did too: 'Lelia cried, Rupert cried, John cried …' Hugh and everyone else in the cast thought it was one of the dramatic high points in the film, but Cassavetes simply cut it – evidence, if any were needed, of how complete was his control over what made it into the final film.

20 A large part of the dialogue in both versions was looped during editing. Some examples: the street fight near the start; the first part of the scene where Ben, Tom and Dennis meet and interact with the three girls; much of the rehearsal hall scene; all of the long shots in the Museum of Modern Art sculpture garden; parts of the scene in which the three boys are playing cards, calling the stewardess and leaving the apartment; Lelia's cry of 'Where are you going?' to Tony when he starts to leave her apartment (which is not even in her own voice); the master shots of groups of people at Hugh's party; and much of the 'happiness boys' pre-fight scene.

21 Jonas Mekas told me that Cassavetes told him he gave the print of the first version to a film school, but it has never been located and has probably been destroyed.

22 Cassavetes himself told me about Aurthur's involvement, which was confirmed by David Pokotilow. Kollmar remembers that Aurthur was present on the set for some of the shooting in the first version, although says he knows nothing about his involvement in the rewrite. The date for the reshoot is my best estimate based on the available evidence.

23 The passage is another illustration of Cassavetes' exaggerations in interviews he gave. He fudges the durations for effect, lengthening the first shoot and shortening the second. As noted previously, the first shoot took ten weeks; the second fourteen days.

24 Cassavetes turns the liability into an asset, though, since the fact that Lelia dances to the same music with both of her boyfriends subliminally knits the film together structurally.

25 Though he had the reputation of being indifferent to the 'look' of his films, Cassavetes would attempt similar 'poetic' effects in many of his later works. Consider the Loser's Club and

Whiskey a Go Go sequences, the 'expressive' shots of Rowlands' face, and the use of different film stocks to capture 'moods' in *Faces*, as well as many shots and scenes in *Minnie and Moskowitz*, *A Woman Under the Influence* and *The Killing of a Chinese Bookie*. The director of the first version of *Shadows* is recognisably the same person who made these films.

26 In re-editing *Shadows*, Cassavetes learned something about the multiplicity of selfhood that he would draw on in all of his subsequent work. He also learned that a film can be massively changed in the editing process – something he would do in every one of his later films.

27 *Shadows*' multiple-strand narrative becomes the template for Cassavetes' later work, which almost always separately presents two or three characters or groups of characters at the start of the film, brings them together for a series of interactions in the middle and separates them again at the end. *Faces* alternates between two sets of characters – those associated with Jeannie's apartment (Richard, Freddie, McCarthy, Jeannie and others) and those associated with the Forst home (Maria, Chettie and Maria's friends). *Minnie and Moskowitz* and *Love Streams* both start with separate stories which subsequently overlap (those of Seymour and Minnie and Robert and Sarah). Even films like *Husbands*, *Gloria* and *Opening Night* which may at first glance seem exceptions to the rule, do something similar – not only employing parallel-editing techniques to shuttle between various strands of a story (as when *Husbands* separately presents Archie's, Harry's and Gus's interactions with various women), but displaying a 'democratic' even-handedness within individual scenes in which 'minor' characters are briefly allowed to take over the narrative. In *Opening Night*, for example, the viewer is always aware of four or five different perspectives on everything. It is interesting in this respect that two of Cassavetes' most commercially successful films, *A Woman Under the Influence* and *Gloria*, are the ones that are the most conventionally organised around 'star' performances – though even these works circulate the viewer among many other points of view.

28 The effect is to create a series of implied parallels. While the Hollywood movie is a vehicle for star turns, Cassavetes' work is an echo chamber of comparisons and contrasts.

29 Given Cassavetes' fondness for De Sica, my guess would be that the moment with the cabby is indebted to any number of similar moments in De Sica's work – most likely the garbage truck ride in *Bicycle Thief*. Every one of Cassavetes' films has similar scenes, where a minor character or characters briefly take centre stage. In *Minnie and Moskowitz*, there are Morgan Morgan, Jim and Zelmo; in *The Killing of a Chinese Bookie*, there are a bartender and waitress at a hamburger joint. Cassavetes' putative 'stars' cannot stand unchallenged even at moments of anguish and high drama.

Although there are apparently similar moments of 'comic relief' in many other films, I would note that there is a fundamental difference between what Cassavetes is doing with the cabby and what these other works generally do. In *Psycho* when Lila and Sam interact with the sheriff and his wife, rather than being genuinely chastened or 'placed' by the comic figure, the perspective of the main characters is reinforced. That is to say, it becomes all the more important that Lila and Sam pursue their quest since they are the only ones who truly understand the problem.

Another false comparison with scenes like the one with the cabby in Cassavetes' work that is frequently proffered is the 'chicken salad sandwich' moment in *Five Easy Pieces*, because the narrative is put on hold for a moment while a little acting riff takes place. But Cassavetes is doing something quite different. He is, in a neorealist vein, genuinely sidetracking his narrative into a new path, while during Nicholson's interaction with the waitress, there is no question that Nicholson's thoughts and feelings are the centre of attention and Nicholson the 'star' of the scene, as much as ever.

30 For more on Cassavetes' acts of visual contextualisation, see my *The Films of John Cassavetes: Pragmatism, Modernism, and the Movies* (Cambridge: Cambridge University Press, 1994), pp. 93–5, 176, 203–12.

31 *Faces* and *Love Streams* illustrate the same point. In both works, the main characters are financially extremely well off, but their wealth matters as little as the poverty of the characters in this film does. Cassavetes is like Henry James in this respect. The financial need of Isabel Archer and the financial security of Maggie Verver exist to create imaginative situations for them to deal with – not financial.

32 Cassavetes' personal statement to the author. He told me that my *American Dreaming* contained the only essay on *Shadows* that he agreed with and that understood this aspect of the film. (Incidentally, Cassavetes' anti-ideological bent is probably the reason he cut Hugh Hurd's 'newspaper' scene from the film. It suggested that the characters' problems were sociological rather than personal.)

33 Lelia has at least as much trouble interacting with Davey Jones as with Tony, and Ben's problems are not with the two white boys he cruises with, but with members of his own family and racial group like Lelia, Hugh and Jackie.

34 Stylistically and ideologically inflected films implicitly freeze characters and relationships into static positions. They de-temporalise experience. Once abstract significances are attached to characters' situations and relationships, they are more or less fixed in one place imaginatively. If a scene is kick-lighted one moment, it will be kick-lighted the next; if the music is suspenseful at the start of a scene it will generally still be suspenseful a minute later. If a character is a representative of a certain ideological situation, he will tend to remain representative.

One might assume that the use of music in *Shadows* would stabilise interpretations around certain moods. However, the jazz scoring functions in a fundamentally different way from standard 'movie music' orchestration. It does not dictate a specific emotional response. And if it even borders on doing that, Cassavetes changes it. This is the case in the concluding sequence of the film, from the fight scene to the boys' conversation in the restaurant to the shots of Ben walking off into the night. Cassavetes

changes the music with each successive scene to prevent the viewer from reclining into a fixed mood.

35 *A Woman Under the Influence*'s Mabel and *The Killing of a Chinese Bookie*'s Cosmo Vitelli display the two alternatives. Mabel shows us what embodied, practical expressions look like, and Cosmo demonstrates how Cassavetes feels about visionary stances and relations.

I have extended discussions of the issues in this and the preceding section in two essays and a book: 'Two Forms of Cinematic Modernism: Notes Toward a Pragmatic Aesthetic', in Townsend Ludington (ed.), *A Modern Mosaic: Art and Modernism in the United States* (Chapel Hill and London: University of North Carolina Press, 2000), pp. 357–415; 'When Mind is a Verb: Thomas Eakins and the Doing of Thinking', in Morris Dickstein (ed.), *The Revival of Pragmatism: New Essays on Social Thought, Law, and Culture* (Durham and London: Duke University Press, 1998), pp. 377–403; and *John Cassavetes: The Adventure of Insecurity* (Boston: Company C, 2000). All three works are available on my web site at: http://www.cassavetes.com.

36 It goes without saying that the mysteries I am describing are entirely different from the acts of mystification in Hitchcock or the Coen brothers. The latter are simply ways of giving interest to characters and events that they would not otherwise possess. The mystification is created by telling a lie or creating a secret, which can always be cleared up by the final shot by revealing the truth. Cassavetes' mysteries have the density and irresolution of the most interesting events in life. They never go away.

37 See David James, *Allegories of Cinema: American Film in the Sixties* (Princeton: Princeton University Press, 1989), pp. 87–90.

38 The character types in *Shadows* show up in Cassavetes' later work. The title characters in *Husbands* represent male versions of Lelia. The main character in *The Killing of a Chinese Bookie* combines Ben's coolness with Hugh's stoicism and Tony's addiction to charm. Robert Harmon in *Love Streams* has aspects of both Ben and Tony in him.

39 Cassavetes' *Faces*, one of the supreme masterworks of American film, is a virtuosic demonstration of this insight.

40 The irony of the editorial enjambment from Hugh's: 'You certainly look like a refined audi-ence ... and I have a couple of refined jokes to tell ...' to the audience's squeals of delight at the club's lowbrow comedy perfectly expresses Cassavetes' sardonicism about the intelligence of audiences.

Learning from Degas and Cézanne. The drama of unbalanced, asymmetrical compositions and energies that won't be confined within the space of the frame

CREDITS

· ·

Shadows

USA
1959

Director
John Cassavetes
Producer
Maurice McEndree
Screenplay
John Cassavetes and Robert
Alan Aurthur, based on a
workshop improvisation
**Cinematographer and
Cameraman**
Erich Kollmar
Supervising Editor
Len Appelson
Editor
Maurice McEndree
Sets
Randy Liles, Bob Reeh
Production Company
Gena Production
Presented by Jean
Shepherd's *Night People*
©John Cassavetes
Associate Producer
Seymour Cassel
Production Manager
Wray Bevins
Production Staff
Maxine Arnolds, Ellen
Paulos, Anne Draper, Leslie
Reed, Mary Anne Ehle, Judy
Kaufman
Assistant Director
Al Giglio
Grip
Al Ruban
Lighting
David Simon
Assistant to Lighting
Cliff Carnell

Saxophone Solos
Shafi Hadi [a.k.a. Curtis
Porter]
Additional Music
Charles Mingus; performed
by Charles Mingus, double
bass; Phineas Newborn and
Horace Parlan, piano;
Jimmy Knepper, trombone;
Dannie Richmond, drums;
Shafi Hadi, saxophone; and
three unidentified other
musicians
Song
'Beautiful' by Jack
Ackerman, Hunt Stevens,
Eleanor Winters
'A real mad chick' by Jack
Ackerman
Sound
Jay Crecco
Recorded at Titra

Cast
Benito Carruthers
Ben Carruthers
Lelia Goldoni
Lelia Carruthers
Hugh Hurd
Hugh Carruthers
Anthony Ray
Tony Russell
Dennis Sallas
Dennis
**Tom Allen [a.k.a. Tom
Reese]**
Tom
David Pokotilow
David
Rupert Crosse
Rupert
Davey Jones
Davey Jones

Pir Marini
Sam, the piano player in the
rock and roll club, rehearsal
studio, and nightclub
Victoria Vargas
Vickie, talks with Lelia
Jack Ackerman
Jack Ackerman, the
impresario
Jacqueline Walcott
Jackie, talks with Ben

Three girls in the bar:
Joyce Miles
talks with Tom
Nancy Deale
talks with Ben
Gigi Brooks
talks with Dennis

Girls at the party:
Lynn Hamilton
Hugh's girlfriend
Joanne Sages
Rupert's girlfriend
Marilyn Clark
'existential psychoanalysis'
Jed McGarvey
'basic precepts'
Greta Thyssen
exotic dancer

Three boys in the fight:
Cliff Carnell
dark sport coat
Jay Crecco
moustache
Ronald Maccone
light sport coat

Bob Reeh
'I love you truly' taxi driver

[*uncredited*]
Sheldon Hackney
Danny Simon
nightclub comedians

Nicos Papadakis
attacks Lelia
John Cassavetes
dancer in the rock and roll
club and Lelia's protector

Maurice McEndree
'Moe-Moe' in Central Park

Seymour Cassel
dancer in the rock and roll
club and punched by Ben in
the 'Charge' scene

Gena Rowlands
chorus girl in the rehearsal
studio and night-club
audience member

John 'Red' Cullers
Jean Shepherd
Ellen Paulos
other night-club audience
members

'Happiness Boys' scene:
Carol Stern
brunette
Carrie Radison
blonde

US Distributor
Lion International Films,
Ltd and subsequently Faces
International Films, Inc.
UK Distributor
British Lion Films, Ltd

1959 35mm blow-up:
81 minutes
7,279 feet
1958 16mm:
60 minutes

Black and White

ALSO PUBLISHED

An Actor's Revenge
Ian Breakwell

L'Âge d'or
Paul Hammond

L'Année dernière à Marienbad
Jean-Louis Leutrat

Annie Hall
Peter Cowie

L'Atalante
Marina Warner

L'avventura
Geoffrey Nowell-Smith

Belle de Jour
Michael Wood

The Big Heat
Colin McArthur

The Big Sleep
David Thomson

The Birds
Camille Paglia

Blackmail
Tom Ryall

Bonnie and Clyde
Lester D. Friedman

Boudu Saved from Drowning
Richard Boston

Bride of Frankenstein
Alberto Manguel

Brief Encounter
Richard Dyer

Das Cabinet des Dr. Caligari
David Robinson

Cat People
Kim Newman

Chinatown
Michael Eaton

Citizen Kane
Laura Mulvey

Double Indemnity
Richard Schickel

Les Enfants du paradis
Jill Forbes

42nd Street
J. Hoberman

"Fires Were Started –"
Brian Winston

The Ghost and Mrs Muir
Frieda Grafe

Greed
Jonathan Rosenbaum

Gun Crazy
Jim Kitses

High Noon
Phillip Drummond

In a Lonely Place
Dana Polan

It's a Gift
Simon Louvish

The Life and Death of Colonel Blimp
A. L. Kennedy

Lolita
Richard Corliss

M
Anton Kaes

The Magnificent Ambersons
V. F. Perkins

A Matter of Life and Death
Ian Christie

Meet Me in St. Louis
Gerald Kaufman

Metropolis
Thomas Elsaesser

Napoléon
Nelly Kaplan

The Night of the Hunter
Simon Callow

La Nuit américaine
Roger Crittenden

Odd Man Out
Dai Vaughan

Olympia
Taylor Downing

Palm Beach Story
John Pym

Pépé le Moko
Ginette Vincendeau

Performance
Colin MacCabe

Queen Christina
Marcia Landy & Amy Villarejo

Red River
Suzanne Liandrat-Guigues

Rocco and his Brothers
Sam Rohdie

Rome Open City
David Forgacs

Sanshô Dayû
Dudley Andrew & Carole Cavanaugh

The Searchers
Edward Buscombe

The Seventh Seal
Melvyn Bragg

Shane
Edward Countryman & Evonne von Heussen-Countryman

Singin' in the Rain
Peter Wollen

Stagecoach
Edward Buscombe

Sunrise – A Song of Two Humans
Lucy Fischer

Taxi Driver
Amy Taubin

Things to Come
Christopher Frayling

Went the Day Well?
Penelope Houston

Wild Strawberries
Philip & Kersti French

The Wizard of Oz
Salman Rushdie

If you would like further information about future BFI Film Classics or about other books on film, media and popular culture from BFI Publishing, please write to:

BFI Film Classics
BFI Publishing
21 Stephen Street
London W1P 2LN

BFI Film Classics '...could scarcely be improved upon ... informative, intelligent, jargon-free companions.'
The Observer

Each book in the BFI Publishing Film Classics series honours a great film from the history of world cinema. With new titles published each year, the series is rapidly building into a collection representing some of the best writing on film. If you would like to receive further information about future Film Classics or about other books on film, media and popular culture from BFI Publishing, please fill in your name and address and return this card to the BFI.[*] (No stamp required if posted in the UK, Channel Islands, or Isle of Man.)

NAME

ADDRESS

POSTCODE

WHICH *BFI FILM CLASSIC* DID YOU BUY?

[*] In North America, please return your card to: Indiana University Press, Attn: LPB, 601 N. Morton Street, Bloomington, IN 47401-3797

21

BFI Publishing
21 Stephen Street
FREEPOST 7
LONDON
W1E 4AN